HORSE EVALUATION

HORSE EVALUATION

A Multibreed Text for Competitive Youth Horse Judges

COLLEEN M. BRADY

PURDUE UNIVERSITY PRESS
WEST LAFAYETTE, INDIANA

Copyright © 2025 by Colleen Brady. All rights reserved.

Cataloging-in-Publication Data on file at the Library Congress.

978-1-62671-240-9 (paperback)

978-1-62671-241-6 (epdf)

978-1-62671-246-1 (epub)

Cover image: 4-H horse judging clinic. Courtesy National 4-H Council.

CONTENTS

Acknowledgments — vii

Introduction — 1
    Colors and Markings 1
    Conformation 10
    Conformation Faults, Unsoundnesses, and Blemishes 14

1. **Judging Halter Classes** — 20
    Key Characteristics to Look for When Judging Conformation 20
    General Conformation Terms 21
    Breed Specific Considerations 23
        Quarter Horse 23
        Hunter in Hand 26
        Arabian 26
        Morgan 28
        American Saddlebred 29
        Tennessee Walking Horse 30
        Draft Horse 31
        Miniature Horse 33

2. **Judging Performance** — 35
    Key Characteristics to Look for When Judging Performance 35
    Judging Guidelines for Specific Classes 38
        English Equitation 38
        English Pleasure (Saddle Seat) 41
        Hunter Hack 43
        Hunter Under Saddle 46
        Plantation Pleasure 49
        Pleasure Driving 50
        Ranch Riding 51
        Reining 54
        Showmanship 60
        Trail 64
        Western Horsemanship 68
        Western Pleasure 70
        Western Riding 73

3. Oral Reasons   **78**
    Philosophy for Giving Oral Reasons   78
    Major Criteria for Reasons   78
    Scoring Oral Reasons   80

About the Author   *85*

ACKNOWLEDGMENTS

I would like to extend my deepest gratitude to several individuals and organizations whose contributions have been invaluable to the creation of this book on youth competitive horse judging.

Thank you to Dr. Kathy Anderson, American Quarter Horse Association judge and University of Nebraska horse judging coach, for her exceptional expertise and guidance. Her insights have greatly enriched the content and quality of this book.

I am also profoundly grateful to the American Paint Horse Association for providing video examples of different classes. These visual aids have been instrumental in illustrating what the performance classes are supposed to look like and are truly one of the unique components that set this judging guide apart from the many others available. A picture (or video) is truly worth a thousand words.

A special thank-you to Dr. Craig Wood from the University of Kentucky for his detailed conformation drawings. His work has provided a clear and accurate reference for understanding horse conformation.

I would like to acknowledge Dr. Mark Russell, past horse judging coach at Purdue University, for creating the original pamphlet that served as the foundation for this judging guide. His work has been a cornerstone in the development of this comprehensive resource, and he has been a vital contributor to all of the iterations that have led to this final version.

Additionally, I am deeply appreciative of my judging team coaches, Dr. Roy Johnson from the University of Minnesota and Dr. John Shelle from Michigan State University. They taught me to appreciate good horses of any breed or discipline and emphasized that horse judging is first and foremost an educational activity. Their wisdom that competition success, although rewarding, is secondary to the lifelong skills and relationships built through participation in the activity has been invaluable.

Thank you all for your invaluable support and contributions.

INTRODUCTION

The ability to evaluate horses is an important skill for participants in many facets of the horse industry. In addition to the opportunity to participate in competitive horse judging, the development of the skill of horse evaluation can lead to judging professionally and being a more effective selector of horses for a variety of uses.

This manual is designed to achieve the following:

1. Provide information on evaluation of conformation of a variety of breeds and for a variety of purposes.
2. Define judging criteria for a variety of classes.
3. Provide terminology for proper description and comparison of horse characteristics.
4. Provide sample reasons.
5. Explain how to give and score reasons and figure placing scores.

Class specifications are provided based on current rule books, which are noted in the manual. However, there are some differences in breed priorities and requirements. It is always a good idea to reference the most current version of the breed/organization rule book/handbook at the beginning of the judging season to make sure you are aware of any changes to the rules.

COLORS AND MARKINGS

Colors and marking are one of the primary ways we use to identify and differentiate horses. Being able to properly describe horses is useful in conversation about horses and is vital in horse judging for properly identifying horses while giving oral reasons.

The basic horse coat colors are listed below. For more information, check out the online course on colors and markings (https://campus.extension.org/enrol/index.php?id=878) from Extension Horses, Inc.:

Appaloosa: A unique spotted pattern. Leopard Appaloosas have spots covering the entire body. Blanketed Appaloosas have a blanket of spots over the rump. Leopard Appaloosas have spots across the entire body. Some Appaloosas are roaned only, and others are solid-colored. Whatever the pattern, mottling of the skin around the muzzle, eyes, and anus is almost always present, as are prominent white around the iris and striped hooves.

Blanketed Appaloosa

Leopard Appaloosa

Bay: Ranges from tan through red to reddish brown. Mane and tail are black. Black is on the lower legs.
Black: True black without light areas. Mane and tail are black.

Bay

Black

Brown: Brown or black with light areas at the muzzle, eyes, flank, and inside upper legs. Mane and tail are brown or black.
Buckskin: Yellowish or gold. Mane and tail are black. Black on the lower legs.

Buckskin

Chestnut: Dark red or brownish red. Mane and tail are the same as body color or flaxen.

Chestnut

Dun: Yellowish or gold. Mane and tail are black or brown. Dorsal stripe. Zebra stripes on legs. Transverse stripe over withers.

Dun, grullo: The grullo is a form of dun that is smoky or mouse-colored. Mane and tail are black. Black dorsal stripe. Black on lower legs.

Grullo

Dun, red: The red dun is a form of dun that is yellowish or flesh-colored. Mane and tail are red or reddish, flaxen, white, or mixed. Red or reddish dorsal stripe. Red or reddish zebra stripes on legs. Transverse stripe over withers.

Red dun

Gray: The gray is a mixture of white with any other colored hairs. Can range from steel gray to rose gray. Usually gets more white as horse ages.

Gray

Palomino: Golden yellow. Mane and tail are white. No dorsal stripe.

Palomino

Pinto: May have any of the basic body colors but in addition has a white pattern superimposed on the color. There are three types.

Pinto, overo: The overo pinto is white and does not cross the topline. One or more legs are dark. Head is often bald-faced. Markings are irregular. Tail is one color.

Overo

Pinto, tobiano: The tobiano pinto has white crosses on the topline. All legs are white. Head has minimal white. Body spots are regular. Tail can be two colors.

Tobiano

Pinto, tovero: The tovero pinto is a combination of the tobiano and overo patterns. A definite pattern does not exist. (It is important to note here the difference between a Paint and a pinto. The American Paint Horse is a stock-type breed that exhibits the pinto color pattern. The pinto is the color pattern and appears in several breeds of horses and ponies. A Paint is a pinto, but a pinto is not necessarily a Paint. It would be inaccurate to define a Saddlebred, or Shetland, with this color pattern as a Paint.)

Roan: Uniform mixture of white and dark hairs on a large portion of the body, usually darker on the head, lower legs, mane, and tail. The roan is properly described based on the color the white hairs are mixed with.

    Roan, bay: The bay roan has a uniform mixture of white on a bay coat with a black mane and tail.

    Roan, blue: The blue roan has uniform mixture of white with black hair.

Blue Roan

Roan, red: The red roan has a uniform mixture of white and red (chestnut) hair. Also known as strawberry roan.

Sorrel: Reddish or copper red. Mane and tail same as body color or flaxen. Most appropriately used when describing stock-type horses.

White: Pure white. Mane and tail white. True white horses are born white. Should be differentiated from gray horses that become whiter with age.

Red Roan

QUALITY OF MOVEMENT

The horse should move with a straight, smooth stride when viewed from the front, the side, or the rear. Desirable length, animation, and cadence of stride will vary with the discipline; however, there are some common flaws in movement that should be noted.

Forging: A defect in the way of going, characterized by the striking of the supporting forefoot by the striding hind foot on the same side.

Interfering: A defect in the way of going, characterized by the striking of the fetlock or cannon of the supporting leg by the opposite foot that is in motion. This condition is more prevalent in horses that toe out in front.

Paddling: The striding foot swings outward, away from the supporting leg. This is most commonly seen in a horse with a toed-in conformation

Rope walking: A twisting of the striding leg around and in front of the supporting leg, resembling a tight-rope walker.
Winging: The striding foot swings inward toward the supporting leg. This is most commonly seen in a horse with a toed-out conformation.

CONFORMATION

Conformation includes balance, type, muscling, and structural correctness and also includes the form and proportion of the various parts of the body.

BALANCE

A balanced appearance comes from the forequarter and hindquarter appearing to be of nearly equal size and development. They "fit" together well. A heavy-fronted horse that is narrow and shallow in the rear quarter is not balanced, nor is a heavy-quartered horse that is narrow, flat, and shallow in front.

When all the parts of the horse blend together well and the muscling is smooth and tapering, the horse is said to have balance. The head and neck should be in proportion, and the neck should blend into the shoulder smoothly. The shoulder and forerib should fit together well. The coupling should be short and strong, which allows for a strong topline and being smoothly tied in the hips.

TYPE

Type is the combination of characteristics that distinguish one breed from another. Usually type is seen in the head, neck, croup, tail set, and movement. Type will vary from breed to breed and should be strongly considered when evaluating halter classes. Although a horse's basic body conformation will vary by breed and intended use (discussed in Chapter 1), all horses should have certain "athletic" structural attributes. The following sections briefly describe some desirable characteristics common to most breeds and types of horses. Refer to the breed sections in this manual and the specific rule books for more details about what is most desired in specific breeds.

HEAD

In general, the head should be well proportioned to the rest of the body, refined and clean-cut, with a chiseled appearance. A broad forehead with great width between the eyes is desired. The face should be straight or slightly concave (dished). The eyes, set wide apart, should be large and clear. The ears should be medium or small and set neatly on the head. The muzzle should be small, the mouth shallow, and the nostrils large and sensitive. The bite should be even, with upper and lower teeth meeting. Each breed emphasizes slightly different characteristics about the head, and these characteristics should be considered when breed classes are judged.

NECK

The head should join the neck at about a 45-degree angle. There should be a distinct space between the jawbone and the neck, called the throatlatch, which should be long and clean-cut. Depending on the breed, the neck should be medium to fairly long, with the headset at a high or moderate level. The neck should be slightly arched, lean, and muscular and should blend into the shoulder smoothly. An underslung (ewe-neck) or heavily crested neck is undesirable.

SHOULDER

The shoulder should be long and set at an angle of 45 to 50 degrees from the withers down to the point of the shoulder. The shoulder should be smooth yet well-muscled. Straight shoulders are usually short and are associated with a short stride and considerable concussion when the front feet hit the ground.

WITHERS

The withers should be prominent, sharp, and well defined, extending well beyond the top of the shoulder. Low, flat withers do not hold a saddle well and restrict movement of the shoulder blades. The properly balanced horse will be level from the withers to the croup or slightly higher in the withers than the croup. When the withers are higher than the croup, the hindquarters are positioned under the body more, allowing more elevation in front and more drive from behind. If the hind quarters are higher than the withers, it is more difficult for the horse to shift its weight to the hind quarters and perform in an athletic manner. It is important to note that young horses do not grow at an even rate and are frequently higher in the wither or the croup during the growing process. However, as a judge, you must evaluate the horse as it is presented that day and not attempt to predict how that horse will look at maturity.

CHEST

The chest is deep and fairly thick. This depth and thickness extend back into the forerib and the barrel. Chest muscles should be well developed and form an inverted V. A deep heart girth and a well-sprung forerib give room for good respiratory and digestive capacity.

BACK, LOIN, AND CROUP

The topline should include a short, strong back and loin; a long, nicely turned and heavily muscled croup; and a well-set tail. The loin (coupling) must be short and very strongly muscled. The loin also lifts the forequarters off the ground when the horse is in motion. The croup should be smooth, long, and well muscled. A short croup shortens a horse's stride, while a long croup gives more power and length to the stride and improves the horse's balance and symmetry. A short, strong topline and a rather long underline combined with a well laid-back shoulder provide the structural framework for free and balanced movement.

HINDQUARTERS

The hindquarters give power to the horse. They should be thick, deep, and well muscled when viewed from both the side and the rear. This muscling shows in thickness through the thigh, the stifle, and the gaskin. The hind legs are muscled both inside and out, with the gaskin well developed down to the hock. The hocks are wide, deep, and clean.

LEGS

There is a great deal to the saying "poor underpinning indicates a poor horse." Normal forelegs viewed from the front are positioned such that an imaginary vertical line falls from the point of the shoulder down through the center of the knee, the cannon, the fetlock, and the hoof.

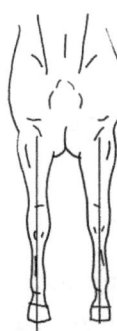

Correct conformation of the front leg from the front view

From the side, a line should fall through the center of the forearm, the knee, the cannon, and the fetlock and should pass just behind the heel.

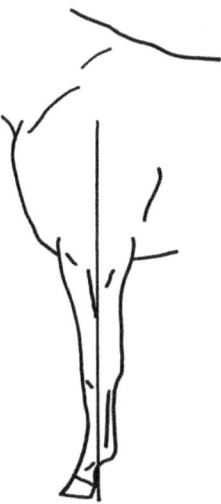

Correct conformation of front leg from the side view

The forearm should be well muscled with broad, flat knees. The cannons should be straight, and tendons should be prominent. A large flexor tendon parallel to the cannon bones constitutes the desired "flat bone." The fetlocks should be large and clean, and pasterns should be moderately long with a slope matching that of the hoof and the toe (about 50 degrees).

The bone structure of the hind legs determines the set of the legs and feet and also affects the arrangement and shape of the muscling of the hindquarters. Correct leg set requires proper bone structure, which is an inherited trait. When viewed from the rear, a line falling from the point of the buttock should bisect the thigh, the gaskin, the hock, the cannon, the fetlock, the pastern, and the hoof.

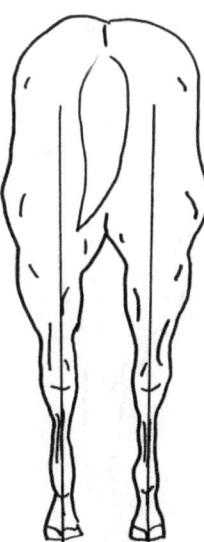

Correct conformation of the hind leg from the rear view

From the side, a vertical line should pass just behind the back of the hock, the cannon, the fetlock, the pastern, and the hoof.

Correct conformation of the hind leg from the rear view

CONFORMATION FAULTS, UNSOUNDNESSES, AND BLEMISHES

Evaluating horses requires the judge to differentiate between conformation faults, unsoundnesses, and blemishes and determine what the impact of each is on the desired use of the horse. A judge must be able to compare the relative importance of each based on either use criteria or class criteria when judging in a show or judging contest. Some common examples of faults, unsoundesses, and blemishes are included below. A *conformational fault* is a deviation from the correct structure of a certain part of the horse. This fault can range from very mild to quite severe, and the severity of the fault will influence how it is considered in a final placement. An *unsoundness* is something that limits the ability of the horse to perform. This can range from something that makes the horse completely unable to perform to something that keeps the horse from meeting its athletic potential. A *blemish* is something that may not be attractive to see, but it does not affect the horse's ability to perform a job.

Back at the knees (calf-kneed or behind at the knees): When viewed from the side, the knee flexes back toward the body. This *conformational fault* puts excessive stress on the carpal joint and the tendons, and affected horses are more likely to develop bowed tendons and knee chips.

Back at the knees

Bench knees: When viewed from the front, the cannons appear to come out of the knee off-center (usually with the cannon on the outside edge of the knee). This *conformational fault* often causes large splints to develop on the inside of the cannon bone. In extreme cases, the knee joint may be offset.

Bench knees

Blindness: This *unsoundness* includes partial or complete loss of vision in either or both eyes, frequently seen as a cloudy white or blue eye. A blind horse usually has erect ears and a hesitant gait.
Blood spavin: This *unsoundness* is a vein enlargement that appears on the inside of the hock and immediately above the depression in the hock. This can cause lameness and damage to the hock.
Bog spavin: This *blemish* is a soft fluid filling under the skin along the natural depression on the inside and front of the hock. A bog spavin is much larger than a blood spavin but is often less serious.
Bone spavin: This *unsoundness* is a bony enlargement on the inside and front of the hock where the base of the hock tapers into the cannon bone. Also called a **jack spavin**, it is a heritable weakness and is one of the most destructive conditions affecting the usefulness of a horse. The lameness is most evident when the horse is worked after resting.
Bowed tendons: An *unsoundess* that results from a thickened, ruptured area of tendons and ligaments (usually the superficial flexor tendon, the deep flexor tendon, and the suspensory ligament) that occupy the space in the back of the cannon region between the knee or hock and the fetlock. Sprains that result in bowed tendons most frequently occur in horses that work at speed and are more commonly seen in the front legs than the rear legs.
Bow knees: Bow-kneed (or bowlegged) horses often stand over the outside of their front feet. This *conformational fault* brings undue weight on the outside portions of the front feet, especially the outside lateral cartilage, often causing formation of **side bones**.

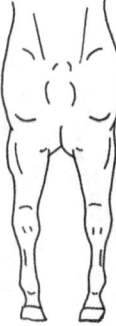
Bow knees (bow-legged in front)

Bowlegged: When viewed from behind, the horse toes in with the hocks turned out. Such horses usually move wide at the hocks with a lateral twist to their hocks, often referred to as rotating the hocks. This *conformational fault* makes collected performance extremely difficult and often causes early unsoundness in the hocks due to the inability to withstand the increased strain.

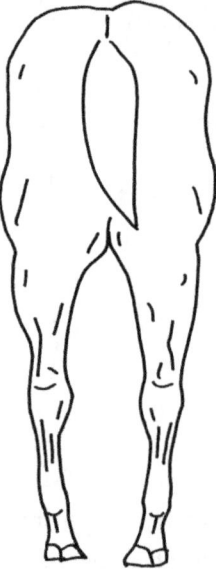

Bowlegged (bowlegged behind)

Capped hocks: A *blemish* where the point of the hock becomes swollen. Capped hocks are usually a result of some trauma to the hock from repeated kicking, hitting the hock point against something, or other similar activities.

Close at the hocks (cow hocks): A *conformational fault* where the hocks turn inward, while the fetlocks and hooves turn outward. A cow-hocked horse moves its hind legs through an inward to outward arc while traveling. It is easiest to see this fault when viewing the horse from the rear.

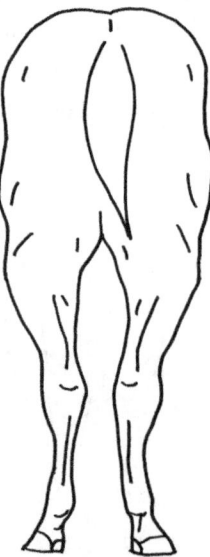

Close at the hocks (cow-hocked)

Curbed hocks or curbs: This *unsoundness* is a condition in which there is fullness on the upper rear of the cannon area about a hand's width below the point of the hock. "Curbs" are due to enlargement of the ligament or tendon and are more prevalent in a horse with too much set to the hock.

Heaves (recurrent airway obstruction): This respiratory *unsoundness* shows as a difficulty in forcing air out of the lungs. It is characterized by a jerking of the flanks (double flank action) during exhaling, and chronic sufferers may develop a "heave line" in their abdominal musculature. **Recurrent airway obstruction** was previously known as chronic obstructive pulmonary.

Hernia or rupture: This *blemish* is a protrusion of any internal organ through the wall of its containing cavity. This usually refers to the protrusion of a portion of the intestine through an opening in the abdominal muscle or a scrotal hernia.

Osselets: An inclusive term referring to a number of abnormal conditions around the fetlock joints resulting in *unsoundness*. Generally, osselet denotes a well-defined swelling slightly above or below the center of the joint and off-center of the exact front of the leg. Affected horses travel with a short, choppy stride and show evidence of pain when the ankle is flexed.

Over at the knees (buck-kneed or knee-sprung): This *conformation fault* is best seen when viewed from the side. The knees flex forward and are not aligned directly under the forearm. Although this trait in unappealing, the knees are not likely to suffer excessive wear.

Over at the knees

Overbite (parrot mouth or overshot jaw): This is a heritable *unsoundness* resulting in the lower jaw being shorter than the upper jaw.

Ringbone: This *unsoundness* is a bony outgrowth involving one or more bones and/or joints of the pastern region. Ringbone primarily affects the forefoot, although the hind foot may be involved. This condition usually causes a progressive lameness, as the bony outgrowth completely encircles, or rings, the pastern region (hence the name "ringbone"). It is usually accompanied by a stiffened ankle if either the pastern joint or the coffin joint is involved.

Roaring: This respiratory *unsoundness* can be identified by a whistling or wheezing that becomes worse as exercise increases. Roaring occurs because of the paralysis of soft tissue in the throat that covers the trachea and decreases airflow. The paralyzed flap can be surgically repaired.

Shoe boil or capped elbow: This *blemish* is a soft fleshy swelling caused by an irritation at the point of the elbow. The two most common causes are injury from the heel calk of the shoe and injury from contact with a hard surface.

Side bones: This *unsoundness* results from the ossification of lateral cartilage of the coffin bone seen protruding immediately above and toward the rear quarter of the hoof head. Shin bones are most commonly in the forefeet, and the condition may occur in one or both feet and on one or both sides of the foot.

Splints: Abnormal bony growths that can occur on the inside and/or outside of the cannon bone. They are most common on the inside of the front leg. When found on the hind leg, they are usually on the outside. Initially they are very painful but eventually become a *blemish* in most cases.

Sweeny: This *blemish* is a depression in the muscle mass of the shoulder caused by an injury to a nerve, resulting in a lack of enervation or control of muscle tone, with subsequent atrophy or muscle degeneration.

Thoroughpin: A *blemish* that is a puffy condition in the hollow of the hock. The puff can be seen mostly on the outside of the hock but is movable when palpated. Thoroughpin rarely causes lameness.

Toed-in (pigeon-toed): In this *conformational fault*, the horse stands with its toes turned inward. Rotation may begin in any point of the leg. Such a horse commonly exhibits paddling as a result.

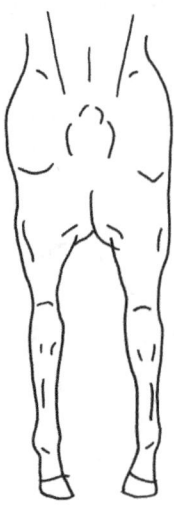

Toed-in (pigeon-toed)

Toed-out (splay-footed): In this *conformational fault* a horse stands with the toes of the front legs turned outward. The horse "wings" when moving, which is when the striding foot swings inward toward the supporting leg.

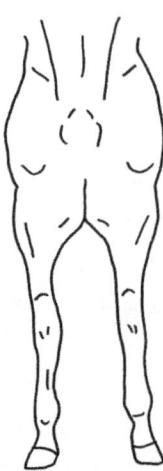

Toed-out (splay-footed)

Too much set to the hocks (sickle-hocked): This is a *conformational fault* that is best seen when viewed from the side. There is excessive angulation in the hock joint. The classic line drawn up the back of the cannon ends behind the point of the buttock. If the angle is too acute, a curb can develop.

Too much set to the hock (sickle-hocked)

Too straight in the hocks (post-legged): This *conformational fault* is best viewed from the side. There is too little angulation in the hocks. The classic line drawn up the back of the cannon ends forward of the point of the buttock, toward the hip. This conformation results in a short, rough stride and excessive wear on the hard tissue in the hock.

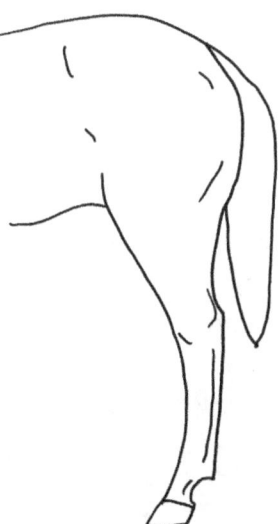

Too straight in the hocks (post-legged)

Underbite (monkey mouth or undershot jaw): This is a heritable *unsoundness* resulting in the lower jaw being longer than the upper jaw.

Windpuff: This *blemish*, also referred to as **windgall**, is a puffy enlargement of the pastern joint. The enlargement is a fluid-filled distention of the bursa.

1

JUDGING HALTER CLASSES

KEY CHARACTERISTICS TO LOOK FOR WHEN JUDGING CONFORMATION

Regardless of breed or type that is being judged, the basic characteristics you look for when assessing conformation are the same. The priority order below is generally applicable to judging all halter classes; however, some specific classes may have some variation in this order based on breed or gender. Refer to the breed-specific sections later in this manual for how these characteristics are prioritized for different breeds.

- Balance
- Structure
- Muscle
- Movement
- Quality
- Sex characteristics
- Breed characteristics

When judging, you should develop your own consistent method of evaluating each horse and comparing it to the other horses in the class. In a judging contest, you will see a horse from a side view, a front view, and a rear view. Below is a recommendation of a process you could use when evaluating. However, with practice you may develop your own strategy.

When you first see the horses, likely from a side view, take a quick note of each of the following:

- Balance
- Breed type
- Sex characteristics
- Color/markings/IDs
- First impression

Once you've created your first impressions and you continue to compare the horses from the side, observe and note the following:

- Balance
- Forehand, middle, and hindquarter assembly (all parts should be correct, proportional, and blend correctly)
- Correctness of feet and legs

As you compare the horses from the front view, observe and note:

- Head quality
- Width of chest/shoulders
- V muscling of chest
- Front leg structure

As you compare the horses from the hind view, observe and note:

- Hind leg structure
- Width of hip
- Muscle expression of inner and outer gaskins
- Width of stifle
- Tail set

As the horses travel, watch as they come toward you and away to see if they are tracking straight. In breeds where quality of movement is an important criterion, you will also want to observe the horse moving from the side to see its length of stride and if it has a flat stride or a stride with a lot of flexion of the knees and hocks. Which movement is most desirable will depend on the class.

When you have an opportunity for close inspection, check for

- Swellings
- Blemishes

GENERAL CONFORMATION TERMS

The following is a list of general conformation terms that can be used for all breeds. The terms listed under the different breed sections are those more suitable to describe the specific type of horse.

- Combined balance, style, and femininity to the highest degree
- Was a stronger profiling individual
- Showed more balance and symmetry
- Was more athletic in his appearance
- Was a smoother blending horse
- Showed more overall balance as the horse . . .
- Showed more desirable type as the horse . . .
- Was a longer-patterned individual
- Ran a higher degree of utility or usefulness

- Exhibited a more correctly angled shoulder, which extended further into the horse's back, thus giving it a shorter, stronger back in relation to a longer, more sloping underline
- Was more equally divisible into thirds
- Was more modern in its design and appearance
- Was more athletic in its muscle expression
- Wrapped a higher volume of muscling around the forearm and gaskin
- Was heavier-muscled from front to rear
- When viewed from the front, stood wider from shoulder to shoulder and V'ed deeper into its chest floor
- When viewed from behind, stood wider from hock to hock
- Showed more breed type in that . . .
- Exhibited a higher degree of substance and style
- Was more prominent about the withers
- Had a shorter and stronger back
- Was smoother over the topline
- Has a stronger topline
- Exhibited a longer, more sloping shoulder
- Was deeper through the heart girth with more spring of rib
- Was deeper in the heart and stifle
- Is more feminine/masculine about the head
- Had brighter, more expressive eyes
- Had a cleaner, chiseled jaw with a smaller muzzle
- Was more alert about the ears
- Cleaner and trimmer in the throat latch
- Had a neck that blended more smoothly from poll to withers
- Had a longer, more slender neck
- Stood wider from shoulder to shoulder on a sturdier column of bone
- Showed more capacity through the barrel
- Had a cleaner underline
- Was stronger and broader across the loin
- Had a more desirable turn to the croup
- Exhibited a more desirable tail set
- Showed more length and development to the hip
- Showed more athletic angle from stifle to hock
- Was deeper in the flank
- Was flatter across the knees
- Stood on flatter, cleaner joints
- Was more structurally correct in underpinning as the horse . . .
- Stood straighter on its front/hind legs
- Showed more substance of bone
- Stood more correctly on all four corners
- Showed more length and slope to pastern
- Traveled straighter and truer

- Tracked more accurately when viewed from behind
- Traveled with more symmetry to its stride
- Traveled with a longer, lighter stride
- Longer, cleaner, and more flexible in its neck
- Was more elegant and refined through the head and neck
- Exhibited a longer, leaner neck that tied higher into the chest

BREED-SPECIFIC CONSIDERATIONS

QUARTER HORSE

AQHA HANDBOOK, 2025

"The purpose of the class is to preserve American Quarter Horse type by selecting well-mannered individuals in the order of their resemblance to the breed ideal and that are the most positive combination of balance, structural correctness, and movement with appropriate breed and sex characteristics and adequate muscling. The ideal American Quarter Horse shown at halter is a horse that is generally considered to be solid in color and possesses the following characteristics: the horse should possess eye appeal that is the result of a harmonious blending of an attractive head; refined throat latch; well-proportioned, trim neck; long, sloping shoulder; deep heart girth; short back; strong loin and coupling; long hip and croup; and well-defined and muscular stifle, gaskin, forearm and chest. All stallions 2 years old and over shall have two visible testicles.

These characteristics should be coupled with straight and structurally correct legs and feet that are free of blemishes. The horse should be a balanced athlete that is muscled uniformly throughout. One of the most important criteria in selecting a horse is conformation, or its physical appearance. Rating conformation depends upon objective evaluation of the following four traits: balance, structural correctness, breed and sex characteristics, and degree of muscling. Of the four, balance is the single most important, and refers to the structural and aesthetic blending of body parts. Balance is influenced almost entirely by skeletal structure."

The head of a Quarter Horse is short and broad with wide-set eyes, large nostrils, a short muzzle, a firm mouth, and well-developed jaws. The head of the Quarter Horse joins the neck with a distinct space between the jawbone and neck muscles to allow the horse to work with its head down and not restrict its breathing. The medium-length, slightly arched full neck blends into sloping shoulders. The good saddle back is created by the horse's medium-high but sharp withers, extending well back and combining with its deep, sloping shoulder.

The Quarter Horse is deep- and broad-chested, as indicated by its great heart girth and wide-set forelegs that blend into the shoulders. The smooth joints and very short cannons are set on clean fetlocks, and the medium-length pasterns are supported by sound feet. The powerfully muscled forearm tapers to the knee, whether viewed from the front or back.

The short saddle back is characterized by being close-coupled and especially full and powerful across the kidney. The barrel is formed by deep, well-sprung ribs back to the hip joints, and the underline comes back straight to the flank.

The rear quarters are broad, deep, and heavy, viewed from either side or rear, and are muscled so they are full through the thigh, stifle, gaskin, and down to the hock. The hind leg is muscled inside and out. When viewed from the rear there is great width extending evenly from the top of the thigh to the bottom of the stifle and gaskin. The hocks are wide, deep, straight, and clean.

The flat, clean, flinty bones are free from fleshiness and puffs but still show much substance. The foot should be well rounded and roomy, with an especially deep, open heel.

QUARTER HORSE TERMS

- Exhibited a more desirable outline
- Was more balanced from end to end
- Was smoother blending
- Showed more type, style, and balance
- Was more athletic in appearance
- Presented more overall balance and symmetry
- Was more expressive about the eye
- Was wider between the eyes
- Exhibited a stronger, more powerful jaw
- Was cleaner and more refined about the head
- Was cleaner through the throatlatch
- Had a longer, more supple neck
- Was smoother blending from neck to wither
- Had a more correctly laid-back shoulder
- Was more prominent at the wither
- Was stronger over the topline
- Was smoother over the croup
- Was deeper through the heart and flank
- Was deeper through the heart girth with more spring to rib
- Exhibited a high volume of muscle about the chest and forearm
- Was more deeply V'ed through the pectoral region
- Was wider from shoulder to shoulder
- Was more expressive in the shoulder and forearm
- Ran a higher volume of muscle from end to end
- Wrapped more muscle around the gaskin
- Was wider from stifle to stifle
- Was more heavily muscled through the hindquarters
- Had more length and carry-down of muscling to the rear one-third
- Exhibited a longer, lower tying muscle pattern
- Stood on a cleaner, flatter column of bone
- More prominent wither that extends further into the back, thus giving the horse a shorter, stronger back in relation to a longer, more sloping underline
- More powerfully muscled through the V of chest
- More powerfully designed as the horse . . .
- Heavier muscled shoulder, arm, and forearm

- Carried a higher volume of muscle
- Longer muscling pattern that was lower in its tying
- More three-dimensional in hindquarter, being longer and more powerful through the hip
- Wider designed at both ends
- Wrapped more total muscle around hind leg to expose a more expansive inner and outer gaskin

SAMPLE REASONS: QUARTER HORSE GELDINGS

I placed the Quarter Horse geldings 1-2-3-4, finding an easy top in 1 who simply overpowered the class in terms of muscle and volume. When viewed from the front, the well-balanced sorrel V'ed deeper into his chest floor and stood wider from shoulder to shoulder, and as I stepped to the profile he was deeper in the heart and stifle with a greater volume of muscling from front to rear. When viewed from behind, he provides a bigger hind leg, being more expressive in his gaskin. Sure, 2 does stand taller at the wither, but he falls into a logical second as he's lighter-built and narrower-made.

Despite these criticisms, 2 most closely follows my class winner in terms of balance and quality, giving him the advantage over 3. Not only does the bay have a longer, leaner neck, but he also has more slope to his shoulder and hip, allowing him to have a shorter, stronger back, thus being more balanced from end to end. There is no question that 3 is wider from stifle to stifle, but he's coarser-fronted and weaker over his topline, so I left him third.

In a poorer-quality bottom pair I used 3 over 4, as the palomino is more structurally correct, standing straighter from knee to toe and from hip to hock to heel. Furthermore, he wraps a greater volume of muscle around a larger, more athletic frame. Today 4, the bay, is my bottom. He is the lightest-made and most structurally incorrect who is rotated in his left cannon, short and steep in pasterns, and travels as well as stands with his hocks behind him. Thank you.

SAMPLE REASONS: QUARTER HORSE MARES

I placed the Quarter Horse mares 2-4-3-1.

In a close top pair, I opted for the added balance I found in 2 over 4. The star-faced bay was more equally divisible into thirds, being shorter and more nearly level from wither to croup while having a more correct turn to her hip. Now, I certainly won't argue that 4 was as clean-fronted and heavy-muscled as any, but she was a notch longer and more uneven over her topline, so I left her second.

Even so, it was 4's combination of quality and muscling that aligned her over 3 in easier intermediate decision. The blaze-faced bay was more feminine about her head and had a longer, cleaner neck that tied higher into her chest. Furthermore, she wrapped a greater volume of muscling around a wider-built frame, especially in her rear one-third, where she had more length and carry-down of muscling. Sure, 3 had a shorter, stronger back, but she falls into third, as she was plainer and coarser-made through her head and neck while also being lighter-muscled and smaller-framed.

Putting these harsh criticisms aside, it's structure and balance that place 3 over 1. Not only did the smoother-blending sorrel lock back more securely in her knees, but she also had a longer, more sloping shoulder that led into a shorter, stronger topline and a more correctly turned croup. There's no doubt that 1 had a cleaner throatlatch, but the light-muscled black finishes the class. She was severely over at the knees as well being the steepest in her shoulder and weakest over her topline, thus having the poorest balance. Thank you.

HUNTER IN HAND

The hunter-in-hand horse has a body that is long and deep-chested, rather narrow, upstanding, and often angular. The horse possesses a high degree of quality and refinement throughout. The head is small, refined, and well-proportioned, with a straight face, small neat ear, and fine throat latch. The neck is long and lean and joins the shoulder smoothly. The shoulders and pasterns are sloping. The cannon bones are relatively short, with long forearms and high-quality bone that demonstrates substance and strength. The thigh and quarter are muscled with long, athletic, powerful, defined muscles. The temperament is active and energetic, and the action is low, efficient, and long-strided. Structural correctness, quality, substance, and soundness are emphasized.

HUNTER-IN-HAND TERMS

- Exhibited a longer, lower hunter frame
- Showed more strength, substance, and balance from end to end
- Stood straighter on all four corners
- Showed more slope from stifle to hock
- Was more athletic and fit in muscle expression
- Was deeper through the heart girth
- Traveled with more reach from his shoulder

SAMPLE REASONS: HUNTER IN HAND

I placed the hunter-in-hand mares 4-3-2-1, starting with the individual that led the class with her overall quality, balance, and type.

In my top pair I placed 4 over 3 as 4 was more elegant and refined about the head and neck with a cleaner, chiseled jaw tapering to a smaller muzzle. She was cleaner and trimmer in the throatlatch with a longer, more slender neck. Furthermore, 4 had a more desirable turn to the croup. I do grant that 3 had a larger, more pleasing eye and a longer, more sloping shoulder. However, it was 4 that stood on cleaner, straighter legs on all four corners.

In my middle pair, I chose 3 over 2, as 3 showed more strength of topline and was shorter and stronger in the back. In addition, 3 was stronger and broader across the loin. I do grant that 2 showed more quality, refinement, and femininity about her head. Nonetheless, it was 3 who was the stronger-profiling individual.

Dropping to my bottom pair, I placed 2 over 1, as 2 was a smoother-blending horse that exhibited more refinement and substance. I faulted 1 and placed her fourth, as she was plain about the head, weak over the croup, and lacked the overall refinement and structure to place higher today. Thank you!

ARABIAN

USEF RULEBOOK, 2025

The head of the Arabian is comparatively small, with a straight or slightly concave (dished) profile. The eyes are large, round, and expressive and set well apart. The distance between the eye and muzzle is short. The ears are small, thin, and well shaped, with the tips curved slightly inward. The neck is long and arched, set high and running well back into moderately high withers. The shoulder is long, sloping, and laid over with plenty of muscle, and the ribs are well sprung. The forearms are broad, with short cannon bones. The loins are broad and strong. The croup is relatively horizontal, and the tail carriage is naturally high and straight when viewed from the rear. The hips are strong and round with well-muscled thighs and gaskins. The pasterns are sloping, and the feet are round and of proportionate size. Transmissible weaknesses must be strongly penalized in breeding stock, and horses must be serviceably sound.

In colt/stallion and filly/mare breeding classes, emphasis shall be placed in the following order of importance: type, conformation, suitability as a breeding animal, quality, movement, substance, manners, and presence. When colt/stallions and geldings are judged together, the above class specification will be used except that geldings shall not be judged on suitability as a breeding animal.

In gelding-in-hand classes, emphasis shall be placed in the following order of importance: conformation, type, quality, movement, substance, manners and presence.

ARABIAN TERMS

- More overall Arabian type
- Stronger and more comparatively horizontal over the croup
- More characteristic about the head
- Had a larger, more expressive eye
- Was cleaner and sharper about the head
- Was more prominent over the withers
- Showed more brilliance and animation at the trot
- Was more refined and stylish about the head
- Had a longer, more graceful neck that came out higher from a more sloping shoulder
- Folds the knees with more elevation and works more aggressively over the hocks
- Longer and smoother muscling through the quarter and gaskin
- Was cleaner about the hocks and knees
- Exhibited greater spring of rib and depth of heart
- Exhibited more style, grace, and overall smoothness
- Was more deeply dished about the head

SAMPLE REASONS ARABIAN STALLIONS

I placed this class of Arabian stallions 1-3-2-4. I started with 1, the bay, as he was the most correct in his combination of quality, type, and balance. In relation to 3, he is more alert and expressive in his ears and eyes, with a more refined muzzle with more flaring nostrils. He is cleaner in his throatlatch with a longer, more shapely neck.

Furthermore, he is more nearly level in his topline and hip, with a more correct tail set.

In my intermediate pair, 3 is a more balanced individual who has a more desirable shape to his neck and a more correctly sloping shoulder that lays into a shorter back. 3 simply is more eye-appealing and exhibits more Arabian type.

Dropping to my final pair, volume and substance place 2 over 4. The black is a more powerfully muscled stallion who is more alert in his expression and longer and leaner in his neck, with a smoother neck-to-wither attachment. He is stronger and more level in his topline, with a more ideal hip shape.

Today 4, the stocking-legged bay, is my bottom. I faulted him and placed him fourth because he lacks the type and quality to place any higher in this class. He is the narrowest-made, poorest-balanced individual who is plain in his head and is the lightest-muscled stallion in this class.

MORGAN

USEF RULEBOOK, 2025

The head of the Morgan should be expressive with a broad forehead; large, prominent eyes; a straight or slightly dished short face; firm, fine lips; large nostrils; and well-rounded jowls. The throatlatch is slightly deeper than that of other breeds yet should be refined enough to allow proper flexion at the poll and normal respiration. The neck should come out on top of an extremely well-angulated shoulder, with depth from the top of the withers to the point of the shoulder. The neck should be relatively fine in relation to sex and is also slightly deeper than that of other breeds. The neck should be slightly arched and should blend far back into the withers and back. The topline of the neck should be considerably longer than the bottom line. The stallion should have more crest than the mare or gelding. The withers should be well defined and extend back in proportion to the angulation of the shoulder. Viewed from the side, the topline represents a gentle curve from the poll to the back, giving the impression of the neck sitting on top of the withers rather than in front of them. The back is short and straight, and the croup is relatively level, rounding into a well-muscled thigh. The tail should be attached high and carried with an arch to it. At maturity, the croup should NOT be higher than the withers. The underline should be long and the body deep through the heart girth and flanks. The extreme angulation of the shoulder results in the forearm being a little more vertical than that of other breeds, placing the front legs slightly farther forward on the body. The legs should be structurally correct. The overall picture of the Morgan should show a combination of muscling and substance with refinement. A good Morgan will display a great deal of attitude and alertness, combined with a great deal of animation in its strong, natural way of going. Horses should be judged both standing square and stretched.

Emphasis is placed on type, conformation, and quality of movement. The walk should be rapid, flat-footed, elastic, and four-beat, with the accent on flexion in the pastern. The trot should be a two beat with diagonal gait, animated, elastic, square, and collected. The hind action should be in balance with the front.

MORGAN TERMS

- More closely matched the standard of perfection set by the Morgan breed
- Showed more substance combined with refinement
- Exhibited greater show-ring presence
- Was a brighter, bolder, and more expressive individual
- Showed more natural thickness and dimension
- More vertical in the way the neck came out of the shoulder
- Neck tied in higher and smoother
- Neck rose more vertically out of the shoulder
- Neck was higher and stronger, coming out of the top of a well-angulated shoulder
- Exhibited higher, rounder motion

- Had a better combination of knee and shoulder action, reaching out farther and breaking over higher with each stride of a bolder trot
- Showed more brilliance and animation in its way of going

AMERICAN SADDLEBRED

USEF RULEBOOK, 2025

The ideal American Saddlebred has a well-shaped head carried relatively high with small, alert, pointed ears set close; large eyes set well apart; a fine muzzle with large nostrils; and a straight face line. His long neck is nicely arched with a fine, clean throatlatch. He has high withers with long, sloping shoulders and a short, level back with well-sprung ribs. The croup is level with a well-carried tail coming out high. The forearms and hindquarters are well muscled to the knees and hocks. Legs are straight, with broad, flat bones; sharply defined tendons; and sloping pasterns. He has good, sound hooves, open at the heels. The average height is about sixteen hands.

Clean, rhythmic, and fluid action is paramount. Action should be straight and true, with extreme knee and hock action desired. Winging, interfering, traveling wide behind, mixing of gaits, and loss of form due to excessive speed should be penalized.

The walk should have an elastic step and be prompt, showy, and alert in manner. The trot is a two-beat gait that should be square and bold, with natural action and brilliant motion of the knees and hocks. This motion of the knees and hocks should be snappy and uniform, with each stride being a duplicate of the previous.

Conformation and adherence to the American Saddlebred type constitutes 50% of the in-hand criteria. The remaining 50% is based on way of going and natural action at the walk and trot. Extremely low-backed horses should be penalized.

SADDLEBRED TERMS

- Had a longer, more graceful neck that came out higher from the shoulders
- Was more comparatively horizontal over the croup
- Was more sloping in the shoulder
- Was longer in the hip
- Exhibited more brilliance and animation at the trot
- Had a higher tail set
- Showed more snap to its knees and drive to its hocks
- Had a more reaching trot
- Showed more roll to its shoulders at the trot
- Was more elastic in its stride
- Was more elegant in its appearance
- Was more elegant in its head and neck
- Was a bolder, more expressive horse on the move

SAMPLE REASONS: SADDLEBRED GELDINGS

I placed the American Saddlebred geldings 2-3-1-4, with a strong-backed horse to start and a pair of weaker toplined horses at the bottom.

In my top pair, I chose to place the bay 2 over 3 because 2 presented the most complete package of strength, balance, and style. 2 is stronger-coupled, longer in the hip, higher in the tail set, and more sloping in the shoulder. Furthermore, 2 moved off with a stronger, more powerful stride and showed more animation both fore and rear. I will readily admit that 3 is a more up-headed horse with more refinement of bone and style throughout, but it is 2 that is a more complete package, with more muscle, substance, strength, and quality of movement from end to end.

Moving on to my middle pair, I more easily placed the liver chestnut 3 over the brown 1 because 3 stands more correctly, with his shoulder more sloping, and is stronger and higher in the back. 3 also is cleaner in the head, wider between the eyes, more arched and graceful in the neck, cleaner-boned, and more refined in the muzzle. I grant that 1 is longer in the croup with a higher tail set, but 3 combined strength over the topline and refinement to a higher degree.

In regard to my bottom pair, I placed 1 over 4 because 1 is much stronger in the back, shorter in the coupling, broader in the croup, more sloping in the shoulder, and more balanced from front to back. I appreciate that 4 is cleaner and more stylish about his head and more prominent in the withers, but it is 1 that is more level over the topline, cleaner in his joints, deeper in his heart girth, and longer in his neck. In addition, 1 more closely follows my top-placed horses in animation and brilliance while moving.

Recognizing that 4, the chestnut, stands structurally correct when viewed from behind and is cleanly chiseled about the head, neck, and withers, I nonetheless fault him and place him last because he is weak and low in the back, with toes out in the front, and lacks the balance, soundness, and presence to place higher in the class today. Thank you!

TENNESSEE WALKING HORSE

The Tennessee Walking Horse should have an intelligent and neat head, well-shaped and pointed ears, clear alert eyes, and a tapered muzzle. The neck should be long and graceful. The shoulders should be muscular and sloping. The back should be short with good coupling at the loins. The chest should be of good proportion and width. The body should be deep in the girth and well ribbed. The croup is generally more sloping than in other breeds. The hips should be well muscled, and this development will usually extend well down toward the hocks. The horse should be from fifteen to sixteen hands in height, with an occasional individual over or under this size. Emphasis shall be placed on type, conformation, substance, and quality.

The flat-footed walk and famed running walk are both basic, loose, four-cornered gaits with a 1-2-3-4 beat, with each of the horse's feet hitting the ground separately at regular intervals (left front, right rear, right front, left rear, left front, . . .). As the horse moves, its head will nod in rhythm with the regular rise and fall of its hooves. Overstriding the track of the front foot with the hind foot—left rear over left front, right rear over right front—is highly desirable. In general, the horse should travel in a straight, direct motion, never winging, crossing, or swinging. The flat walk should be loose, bold, and square with plenty of shoulder motion. The running walk should be executed also with loose ease of movement, pulling with the front feet and pushing and driving with the hind feet. Animation and brilliance in motion is preferred, but accuracy and purity of gait is paramount.

TENNESSEE WALKING HORSE TERMS

- More accurate, four-beat walk
- More rhythm and depth to the head nod

- Longer overstride and deeper hock engagement
- Stronger over the coupling with a longer, more sloping hip
- A more up-headed horse with a deeper, stronger body
- Was more gaited and steadier in its head movement
- Was higher in the neck-to-shoulder junction
- Was more powerful in its rear-quarter muscles and drive
- Was deeper-bodied and a more powerfully muscled horse
- Was a deeper-bodied, stronger horse with a deeper set to the hip
- Showed more elevation in the way the neck rose out of the top of a set of more angulated withers

SAMPLE REASONS: TENNESSEE WALKING HORSE

I placed the Tennessee Walking Horses 4-2-3-1, finding a strong, deeper-bodied pair of bays in the top pair and a bottom horse that was weak throughout and paced when he moved.

In my top pair of bay horses, I placed 4 over 2 because 4 was stronger in the back and rear quarter, had a neck that rose higher out of a more sloping shoulder, and was straighter and truer in his front legs and feet. In addition, 4 was longer in his overreach when walking and deeper in his head nod. I grant that 2 was deeper in the heart girth, cleaner in the head, larger in the eye, and straighter in the hocks, but it was 4 that had the movement, strength of topline, and muscle to be placed first.

In moving to my middle pair, 2 over 3, I found that 2 was a much stronger-bodied gelding with a deeper heart girth, more spring of rib, more expression of muscle in the shoulder and coupling, and a longer, more driving hip that sunk lower with each stride. In addition, 2 was much trimmer about the head and much deeper in the heel. I realize that 3 was a taller, longer-necked horse that moved out well, but 2 was squarer and more balanced in his walk and stronger-bodied throughout.

In regard to my bottom pair, I easily placed 3 over the smaller, pacey 1 because 3 was more sloping in the shoulder, longer-muscled, and more balanced from withers to croup. 3 was more accurate in his four-beat walk with more diagonal movement and was a larger, taller horse with a stronger back. I grant that 1 was more correct in his knees and was longer in the hip, but it was clearly 3 that had more muscle and size and a more accurate and desirable way of going.

Realizing that 1 was straight in his legs and refined in the head, I nonetheless placed him last because he paced on the move and was long-backed, shallow-bodied, high in the tail set, higher at the croup than the withers, and lacked the type, size, and gait to be placed any higher in the class today. Thank you!

DRAFT HORSE

All draft-type horses are characterized by their great massiveness. Power rather than speed is desired. In order to possess this power, the draft horse should be blocky or compact, low-set or short-legged, and sufficiently heavy to enable it throw the necessary weight into the collar to move a heavy load and at the same time maintain secure footing. This calls for a horse around sixteen to seventeen hands in height and weighing not less than 1,600 pounds. Draft horses represent the ultimate in power type. They possess a deep, broad, compact, muscular form suited to the pulling of a heavy load at the walk. A draft horse should have plenty of size, draftiness, and substance. The head should be shapely and clean-cut. The chest should be especially deep and of ample width. The topline should include a short, strong back and loin with a long, nicely turned, and well-muscled croup and a well-set tail. The middle should be wide and deep, and there should be good depth in both fore and rear flanks. Muscling should be heavy throughout, especially in the forearm and gaskin. The shoulder should be sloping. The legs should be straight, true, and squarely set, and the bone should be strong, flat, and show plenty of quality. The pasterns should be sloping, and the feet should be large and should have adequate width at the heels and toughness in conformation. With this draft type, there should be style, balance, and symmetry; an abundance of quality; an energetic yet manageable disposition; soundness; and freedom from disease. The action should be straight and true, with a long, swift, and elastic stride at both the walk and the trot.

DRAFT HORSE TERMS

- Exhibited more mass, volume, and substance
- Was a blockier, more compact individual
- Was a deeper, broader, more compact horse
- Showed more strength and substance throughout
- Showed more suitability to work
- Stood wider when viewed from front to back
- Showed more capacity to the barrel and heart girth
- Had a larger span across the hoof
- Had more depth to the heel
- Stood on a stronger, flatter column of bone
- Stood on a higher-quality underpinning
- Was deeper and more angular in the shoulder and had more depth and volume throughout
- Possessed more snap and elevation of the knees and hocks when on the move

SAMPLE DRAFT HORSE REASONS

I placed this class 2-4-3-1, starting with the individual that topped this class of Belgian Mares with the most complete picture of muscling, balance, and type.

    Drawing your attention to my top pair, I placed 2 over 4, as 2 showed greater depth throughout, being deeper through the heart girth and thicker in the hindquarters, thus enabling her to have more power when tracking. 2 showed a shorter, stronger back in relation to a longer underline and exhibited a more correct turn over the croup. I do realize that 4 was cleaner through the throatlatch; however, it was 2 that displayed a more correct angulation to her shoulder.

    In discussing my middle pair, I chose 4 over 1, as 4 more closely followed the standards set by my top individual as she, when viewed from the profile, was more balanced throughout, being smoother-blending from front to rear. 4 ran a higher volume of muscling from end to end, wrapping more muscling around the inner and outer gaskin. I do grant that 1 showed a more desirable shape to her neck; nonetheless, it was 4 that was fuller through her hip.

    Continuing to my bottom pair, I placed 1 over 3, as 1 exhibited more overall Belgian type by presenting a cleaner, sharper head complemented by a wider, more alert eye. Furthermore, 1 was stronger over the topline. I do appreciate that 3 is more up-headed; however, I chose to leave 3 at the bottom, as she is longer and weaker in the back and lacks the overall substance and balance to place higher today. Thank you!

MINIATURE HORSE

AMHA RULEBOOK, 2025

The American Miniature Horse is a beautiful, small, well-balanced horse that, if all reference to size were eliminated, would have the same conformational proportions of other full-sized light breeds. The mares demonstrate refinement and feminine qualities. The mature stallions show boldness and masculinity. The general impression is to be a balanced individual regardless of size with symmetry, strength, agility, and alertness. Movement is strong, natural, and athletic. In motion the horse will exude athleticism, as demonstrated by suppleness of the shoulders and engaged hocks. In judging when characteristics are almost equal, preference must be given to the smaller horse. Any coat color, pattern, white markings, and eye color are equally acceptable. The head is beautiful, triangular in shape and comparatively small in proportion to the length of the neck and the body. The forehead is broad with large, prominent eyes. The eyes are set well apart and are placed approximately one-third the distance from the poll to muzzle. The distance between the muzzle and the eyes is comparatively short. A profile may be straight or slightly dished below the eyes, blending into large nostrils on a small, refined muzzle. The neck is set on the top of a well-angulated shoulder, departing well above the point of the shoulder and blending into the withers, giving the impression of the neck sitting on top of the withers rather than in front of them. The slender neck is slightly arched, forming a gentle curve from the poll to the back. Its length is in proportion to body, with the topline being considerably longer than the bottom line. The throatlatch is clean and well defined, allowing flexion at the poll and normal respiration. The shoulders are muscular, long, sloping, and well angulated (45–50 degrees), allowing for a free swinging stride and alert head/neck carriage. The body is compact, with a short back, close coupling, broad loins, a deep flank, and well sprung ribs. The back has a long, level, well-muscled croup and is smoothly rounding at the hip. The tail is well set. The underline of the body should be long but not tucked up at the flank. At maturity, the top of the hip must not be higher than the withers. The chest is medium width, with defined muscular development. The legs appear longer than the body is deep. These horses possess flat bone and an appearance of overall substance with refinement. Legs are structurally straight and parallel when viewed from the front and back, with hooves pointing directly ahead. Any color and marking patterns as well as any eye color are equally acceptable. Horses are to be shown in hand at the walk and trot. Horses must also be viewed in motion from the side and judged on the priority conformation, quality, presence, way of going, and type.

MINIATURE HORSE TERMS

- Possessed the most expressive and functional athletic muscle design over a more ideally sized skeletal frame
- Was a smaller, more proportional individual
- Exhibited more overall balance and style
- Possessed more miniature breed characteristics in terms of frame size and overall appearance
- Showed more femininity/masculinity
- Stood straighter on all four corners

SAMPLE REASONS: MINIATURE HORSE

I placed this class 1-2-3-4 starting with the individual that dominated the class of Miniature Stallions with his overall type, style, and balance.

Drawing your attention to my top pair, I placed 1, the gray, over 2, the sorrel, as 1 was cleaner and more sharply chiseled about the head, showing a more prominent dish with a more delicately tapered muzzle, featuring a more widely flared nostril.

Furthermore, 1 was tighter through the throatlatch with a longer, leaner, more gracefully arching neck, which tied in both higher and smoother into a more correctly sloping shoulder. I do realize that 2 showed a higher degree of masculinity throughout; however, it was 1 who showed more overall Miniature Horse style.

In discussing my middle pair, I chose 2 over 3, the pinto, as 2 exhibited greater substance from front to rear. In addition, 2 was more structurally correct, as he stood on a cleaner, flatter column of bone. I do grant that 3 was straighter over the topline; nonetheless, it was 2 that was typier about the head.

Continuing to my bottom pair, I placed 3 over 4, as 3 showed a longer, leaner neck and was more horizontal over the back, loin, and croup. I do appreciate that 4 was deeper through the heart girth; however, I chose to leave 4 at the bottom, as he was long in the face and thick in the neck and lacked the overall type to place higher today. Thank you.

2

JUDGING PERFORMANCE

KEY CHARACTERISTICS TO LOOK FOR WHEN JUDGING PERFORMANCE

Although there is much variation in performance classes that you may be asked to judge at a judging contest or at a horse show, there are a few things that apply across all classes. As each horse enters the arena, the judge should identify the following general items, regardless of specific performance class:

- Is the horse sound? Although in a judging contest contestants are often told to judge all halter horses as sound, in a performance class, where all of the contestants are judging the horses at the same time, you will typically judge horses as they go. And horses that are unsound need to be placed at the bottom of the class.
- First impression: Does he appear appropriate for the class or show-ring ready?
- Is the equipment satisfactory?
- Identify the horse/rider combination. Color, markings, and distinctive attire of the rider can all assist in remembering the horse.
- Where does the horse carry its head and neck?
- How much restraint, control, rein contact, cueing, etc. is required from the rider?
- What is the horse doing with its mouth, eyes, ears, and tail?
- Does the horse exhibit a flat-footed walk and show a true four-beat gait?
- Does the horse maintain a correct rail position?
- Is the horse's speed acceptable and appropriate for the style of riding?

As the horse is asked to jog or trot, consider the following:

- Is the horse smooth in its transition from the walk?
- Does the horse perform true gaits, with desirable rhythm and cadence?
- Is the horse under control with little resistance?
- Is the horse consistent about its speed, head set, etc.?
- Does the horse appear to be coordinated?
- Does the horse have a clean foot pickup and soft foot-to-ground contact?

- Does the horse move with class and style and have correctness about leg flexion and extension?
- Does the horse appear to be responsive and agile in its maneuvers?

When the horse is asked to lope or canter, evaluate these factors:

- Has the horse taken the correct lead?
- Does the horse present a true three-beat gait with rhythm and cadence?
- Does the horse promptly make the transition when requested?

After the horse has executed all three gaits to the left, it will be asked to reverse. Does the horse

- Reverse with ease?
- Display control?
- Reverse correctly?

When judging, continue to appraise the horse's ability at all three gaits to the right in the same manner that was used previously.

When the horse is asked to line up and back, it should

- Stand quietly in the line
- Back promptly in a straight line with its mouth closed.
- Maintain its head position.

When making your final decision, confirm that all horses completed all of the requirements of the class, and then add for difficulty in level of performance and subtract for substandard performance. If there are horses that did not complete all of the requirements (e.g., never loped/cantered on the left lead), they should be placed below horses that did complete all of the class requirements. The level of performance expected should be based on the priorities of the class. Be sure you are aware of what the priorities are. For example, if a class is defined as a youth or amateur pleasure class, manners are a higher priority than in an open pleasure class. Be as objective as possible when placing the class, and be aware of your personal biases that may influence your final placing.

GENERAL PERFORMANCE TERMS

- Movement, manners, consistency
- Quality of motion
- Cadence and rhythm
- Control, correct, collection, coordination, complete
- Relaxed, consistent
- Had more suppleness
- Had more riding quality
- Had a more pleasing form

- Appeared more suitable for the class
- Was more consistent in his rail positioning
- Showed a higher degree of control
- Showed more mechanics of motion
- Had a more balanced action
- Showed more style
- Appeared more relaxed and responsive
- Had more quality of motion
- Was more responsive to the rider's cues
- Showed more cadence and collection at all three gaits
- Showed more lateral flexion
- Had a more pleasing attitude
- Was smoother in its transitions
- Was a more stylish and fluid mover
- Was solid, steady, and honest
- Was more correct in its gaits
- Gave a more polished and stylish performance
- Showed a higher degree of responsiveness
- Was freer from errors
- Exhibited fewer mistakes, thus required less handling
- Took and maintained its gaits in a more correct manner
- Was fresher moving
- Was more willing to work
- Exhibited a smoother way of going
- Had more presence
- Was calmer
- Maintained its gaits, showing less anticipation of cues
- Traveled straighter down the rail
- Was quicker to make transitions through the gaits
- Worked more quietly
- Was more responsive to its rider, picking up both leads quickly and more correctly and going both ways in a quieter fashion
- Was more extended and freer moving in the . . .
- Backed more readily
- Showed less resistance in the mouth when asked to back
- Was more fluid in transitions
- Was cleaner moving
- Was softer moving
- Was steadier in its gaits
- Was more rhythmic
- Had more show ring presence
- Was more pleasing in its ear and eye expressions

- Gave a more honest and steady performance, or ride
- Moved with a more natural stride
- Was a fresher, crisper mover
- Was a cleaner mover
- Had a more rhythmic stride
- Was a more even-strided individual
- Had a more balanced action
- Had more forehand suppleness
- Was lighter on its forehand
- Showed a higher degree of control
- Had a more correct head set
- Was more relaxed through the neck and jaw, while maintaining more attentiveness about its head and ears
- Had a steadier head carriage
- Worked straighter through the bridle
- Showed less stiffness to its poll
- Showed more shoulder, arm, and forearm freedom
- Was more elevated in its shoulder, allowing more freedom of stride in front
- Was more correct in shoulder placement when asked to bend
- Had more drive off its hocks
- Engaged its hindquarters with greater drive and impulsion
- Moved deeper underneath its body
- Was driving with more impulsion from behind

DISQUALIFICATION

Unlike in a horse show, in a judging contest all horses must be placed. If something occurs that would result in disqualification, move the horse to the bottom of your placing but continue to judge, as more than one horse may be disqualified. This is especially important in scored/pattern classes, where each horse performs individually and an error of pattern can result in a disqualification.

JUDGING GUIDELINES FOR SPECIFIC CLASSES

ENGLISH EQUITATION

AQHA HANDBOOK, 2025

Equitation is a class in which the saddle seat or hunt seat rider and his ability to control his horse are judged. The rider should have a workmanlike appearance and light and supple seat and hands, conveying the impression of complete control.

Hand position: Both of the riders hands should be over and in front of the horse's withers, with knuckles 30 degrees inside vertical and hands slightly apart, making a straight line from the horse's mouth to the rider's elbow. This is true in both hunt seat and saddle seat equitation. The method of holding the reins is optional, and the bight of the reins may fall on either side. However, all reins must be picked up at the same time.

Basic body position: The eyes should be up and the shoulders back. Toes should point in a relative forward position, with ankles flexed, heels down, and the calf of the leg in contact with the horse and slightly behind the girth. The ball of the foot is placed in the stirrup iron with weight on the ball of the foot.

Position in motion: At the walk or slow trot, the body should be vertical. At the posting trot, the body should be inclined slightly forward in hunter equitation and remain vertical in saddle seat equitation. The rider should rise in the post when the outside front leg is reaching forward and change diagonals smoothly in pattern work. At the canter, the body should be at a position halfway between that of the walk and the posting trot in hunter equitation. At the gallop or over fences, the body should be more inclined than at the posting trot. The saddle seat rider will maintain the vertical body position at all gaits. Excessive pumping of the legs or the arms should be penalized.

Mounting and dismounting: To mount, take the reins in the left hand and place the hand on the withers. Grasp the stirrup leather with the right hand, insert the left foot in stirrup, and mount. To dismount, the rider may either step down or slide down. The size of the rider must be taken into consideration.

Scoring: Exhibitors are to be scored from 0 to infinity, with 70 denoting an average performance. Patterns will be divided into 6 to 10 maneuvers, as specified by the judge, and each maneuver will be scored from +3 to –3, with 1/2 point increments acceptable that will be added or subtracted from 70.

Maneuver scores should be determined independent of penalties and should reflect equal consideration of both performance of the exhibitor's pattern and the form and effectiveness of the exhibitor and presentation of horse to result in the following scores:

+3 Excellent
+2 Very good
+1 Good
0 Average or correct
–1 Poor
–2 Very poor
–3 Extremely poor

Exhibitors' overall form and effectiveness should also be scored from 0 to 5, with 0 to 2 average, 3 good, 4 very good, and 5 excellent. Exhibitors should also be judged on the rail and their final placing adjusted accordingly.

PENALTIES
3 Points

- Break of gait at the walk or trot up to two strides
- Over or under turn from 1/8 to 1/4 turn
- Tick or hit of cone
- Missing a diagonal up to two strides in the pattern or on the rail

5 Points

- Not performing the specific gait or not stopping within ten feet (three meters) of designated location
- Missing a diagonal for more than two strides in the pattern or on the rail
- Incorrect lead or break of gait at the canter (except when correcting an incorrect lead)
- Complete loss of contact between rider's hand and the horse's mouth
- Break of gait at walk or trot for more than two strides
- Loss of iron
- Head carried too low and/or clearly behind the vertical while the horse is in motion, showing the appearance of intimidation
- Obviously looking down to check leads or diagonals

10 Points

- Loss of rein
- Missing a diagonal for more than two strides in the pattern or on the rail
- Use of either hand to instill fear or praise while on pattern or during rail work
- Holding saddle with either hand
- Spurring or use of the of crop in front of the girth
- Blatant disobedience including kicking, pawing, bucking, and rearing

Disqualification

- Failure by exhibitor to wear the correct number in a visible manner
- Willful abuse of horse or schooling
- Fall by horse or exhibitor
- Illegal use of hands on reins
- Use of prohibited equipment
- Off pattern, including knocking over or being on the wrong side of a cone or marker; never performing designated gait, lead, or diagonal; over or under turning more than 1/4 turn

ENGLISH EQUITATION TERMS

- Presented the most desirable picture of a horse and rider working in unison, as the rider was a more effective and showed the horse to its fullest potential
- Maintained a picture of confidence and control
- Sat taller in the saddle, riding with more style and confidence
- Maintained a smoother and more controlled ride throughout the class
- Carried her or his head up and was more alert, attentive, and confident
- Sat deeper in the saddle, with her or his weight more evenly distributed
- Was quieter and deeper-seated
- Was squarer, with the shoulders and correctly positioned in the lower back

- Maintained a straighter line from shoulder through hip to heel
- Drew a straighter line from shoulder to hip to heel
- Had more stable and educated hands
- Maintained a horizontal line from bit to elbow
- Showed smoother and more effective execution of the aids, demonstrating more adaptability, sympathy, and control with the hands
- Had a more secure leg that maintained closer contact with the sides of the horse, allowing the rider to be discrete with her or his aids
- Had a stronger, more effective leg with more angulation to the heel
- Was easier and more fluid posting at the trot
- Was more functionally correct, maintaining correct diagonals at the trot and correct leads at the canter
- Stayed with the horse and sat transitions more smoothly

SAMPLE REASONS: ENGLISH EQUITATION

I placed the English equitation 3-4-1-2. In a top pair of riders who worked more in unison with their horses, it's 3's advantage in rider position that sorts her to the top. The lady on the gray sat taller and more confident in the saddle while maintaining a deeper seat, all the while drawing a straighter line from shoulder to hip to heel, allowing her to maintain a more stationary lower leg and be more discrete with her cues. Now, I won't argue that 4's horse backed straighter. However, he falls into a logical second, as he was heavier-handed and shallower in his heels, causing him to have more movement in his lower leg and be more obvious with his aids and cues.

Even so, it's 4 who has the clear advantage in horse and rider communication over 1. The gentleman on the black more successfully guided his more willing horse through the pattern, allowing him to draw a more precise pattern and be more correct in the placement of his transitions. Sure, 1 may have had a deeper heel, but the girl on the resistant sorrel must go third, as she receives a major fault for failing to pick up the canter within ten feet of the designated area.

Putting these criticisms aside, it's a matter of disqualification that places 1 over 2. To keep it brief, 1 simply performed the final forehand turn in the correct direction. There is no doubt that 2 more effectively communicates with her horse to draw a more precise pattern, but she takes herself out of the running when she turns the incorrect direction at the end of the pattern for a disqualification. Thank you.

ENGLISH PLEASURE (SADDLE SEAT)

The English pleasure horse is to be shown at a walk, trot, and canter with a light but still rein. Horses are judged on manners, performance, quality, and conformation. Horses may be asked to back, and perform extended trot (strong trot or road trot) or hand-gallop. The walk should be four-beat, flat-footed, brisk, and elastic and have good reach. The pleasure, or normal, trot is a two-beat diagonal gait that is square, cadenced, collected, balanced, and free-moving. Credit is given to horses that maintain cadence and collection with additional animation and brilliance. The strong trot, or road trot, is also two-beat, cadenced, and square, but longer-strided and more ground-covering. This trot is to be performed at a speed that allows a balanced, lengthened stride with moderate collection, without becoming strung out or sacrificing form for speed. Excessive speed and loss of control should be penalized.

The canter is a three-beat gait that should be smooth, moderately collected, unhurried, correct, and straight on both leads. The hand-gallop is an extension of the canter and should show true lengthening and extending of the stride, not just increased speed. Excessive speed and loss of control will be penalized. Horses must show a willingness to move forward at all gaits. Depending on the breed, this may also be called a three-gaited class. The basic judging criteria would remain the same.

ENGLISH PLEASURE TERMS

- Was more brilliant and animated in its action
- Exhibited more show-ring presence and attitude
- Wore the bridle with more elegance and pride
- Was more vertical with its face
- Was a more up-headed individual
- Was prouder in the head and tail carriage
- Was more two-beat and diagonal in the trot
- Was freer and more three-beat in the canter
- Trotted more nearly level
- Was more vertical in knee and hock action
- Exhibited higher and rounder action
- Showed more collection and consistency
- Traveled with a bolder stride
- Showed more drive off of the hocks

SAMPLE REASONS: ENGLISH PLEASURE

I placed this class of Morgan English pleasure 4-2-3-1, feeling that the class presented itself with clear top and bottom pairs. In my top pair, I placed the chestnut 4 over the dark bay 2, as 4 presented himself with more overall style and correctness of gaits. He performed with a truer, more four-beat, flat-footed walk and showed more vertical action in his knees and hocks, exhibiting more brilliance and animation at the trot. I will grant that 2 moved on a softer rein and was quicker in his transitions, but it was 4 that dominated the class with his presence and style.

Moving to my middle pair of bays, I placed 2 over 3, as 2 more closely followed my top horse in terms of style and movement. He was more flexed through his poll, wearing his bridle with more pride and elegance. Furthermore, he was more rounded over his topline and showed deeper hock engagement. I readily admit that 3 backed more readily on command and presented more willingness to respond to the rider's cues, but it was 2 that was a smoother, more balanced, freer-moving horse.

Coming to my bottom pair, I used the bay 3 over the gray 1, as 3 performed with more consistency throughout the class. He was more alert and responsive to his rider, allowing for a more pleasurable ride with smoother transitions, and was straighter and truer on both leads. Realizing that 1 was a more up-headed individual and moved out with boldness in each stride of the trot, I nonetheless fault him and place him last, as he was slow and unresponsive in his transitions, missed his right lead, and lacked the overall consistency, manners, and quality of movement to be placed any higher in the class today. Thank you!

HUNTER HACK

AQHA HANDBOOK, 2025

The hunter hack horse should move in the same style as a working hunter. The class will be judged on style over fences, even hunting pace, flatwork, manners, and way of going. Placing for the class shall be determined by allowing a minimum of 70 percent for individual fence work and a maximum of 30 percent for work on the flat. Faults over fences will be scored as in the working hunter class. Horses eliminated in the overfence portion of the class shall be disqualified.

SCORING GUIDELINES

Scoring over fences shall be on a basis of 0 to 100, with an approximate breakdown as follows:

- 90–100: An excellent performer and good mover that jumps the entire course with cadence, balance, and style.
- 80–89: A good performer that jumps all fences reasonably well or an excellent performer that commits one or two minor faults.
- 70–79: The average to fair mover that makes no serious faults but lacks the style, cadence, and good balance of the scopier horses. Also the good performer that makes a few minor faults.
- 60–69: Poor movers that make minor mistakes and fair or average movers that have one or two poor fences but no major faults or disobedience. Cross canter or no change (60), extra stride in a measured line (61–64), multiple distance mistakes, rail on lip of cup/displaced rail.
- 50–59: A horse that commits one major fault, such as a hind knockdown, refusal, trot, or cross canter or drops a leg.
- 30–49: A horse that commits one major fault, including front knockdowns and refusals, or jumps in a manner that otherwise endangers the horse and/or rider.
- 10–29: A horse that avoids elimination but jumps in such an unsafe manner as to preclude a higher score.

Elimination for the following:

- Third refusal, runout, bolting on course, extra circle, showing an obstacle to a horse, or any combination of these
- Jumping an obstacle before it is reset
- Bolting from the ring
- Failure to keep the proper course
- Jumping obstacles not included on the course
- Falling of horse and/or rider

Faults (to be scored accordingly but do not necessarily cause disqualification during rail work):

- Being on the wrong lead and/or diagonal at the trot
- Excessive speed (any gait)
- Excessive slowness (any gait)
- Breaking gait
- Failure to take the called-for gait when asked
- Head carried too low or too high

- Nosing out or flexing behind the vertical
- Opening mouth excessively
- Stumbling or falling

HUNTER HACK TERMS

- Was more relaxed in its courtesy circle
- Stayed more evenly between the reins
- Was more relaxed and attentive in its approach to the first fence
- Maintained a more even pace down the line
- Was more direct in its approach to its first fence
- Placed its jumps more evenly between the standards
- Was more correct down the line, as the horse did not change leads
- Jumped more evenly off both hind legs
- Jumped with more hindquarter impulsion
- Exhibited greater tuck to its front legs, with higher and more even knees
- Was more preferred in its frame while jumping
- Jumped with a rounder frame, having a more preferred arc
- Had a smoother lead change following its second fence
- Extended more in its hand-gallop
- Was more relaxed at the halt
- Displayed a greater ability to relax and recover when the rider dropped the reins
- Jumped with a tighter tuck to its hock, twisting less behind over the fences
- Was a more hunter-connected horse who exhibited more self-carriage, maintaining a more preferred frame and pace during its fence work as he . . .
- Approached the fences with a longer, more sweeping stride and more drive from behind, and was more preferred in its frame, tucking its knees tighter and more evenly over the fence
- Required less adjustment to take the fence
- Showed less hesitation prior to its takeoffs
- Was more symmetrical over the fence
- Had more tuck to its knees
- Remained straighter between the standards
- Approached the first fence in stride and crossed more near to the center of the fence
- Crossed the center of each fence
- Was more balanced in its stride to and from fences
- Was problem-free down the line and was the most broke individual on the rail
- Was tighter in its undercarriage, more horizontal in its forearm, and more even in its knees
- Was more effective in folding its knees and hocks
- Had more arc to its spine from wither to croup
- Covered the course with a longer, more flowing stride
- Had more style over the fences
- Had more correct jumping form

- Met the fence with less stride interruption
- Met the fences with more rhythm
- Approached the fences in a squarer fashion
- Was more rounded in its spine, thus creating more symmetry to its jumps
- Expressed more willingness and was freer from refusals/hesitations
- Had more hindquarter impulsion in its takeoffs
- Exhibited a more even hunting pace throughout the course
- Approached the fences with a longer, more sweeping stride and had more drive from behind
- Was more correct in the point of departure, pushing off more evenly with its hind legs
- Forearms were more horizontal, with higher knees and a tighter tuck to the lower leg
- Pushed off of its hocks more effectively, providing more drive over the fences
- Had more scope over the fences
- Was more correct in its takeoffs, rating his fences more efficiently
- Met the fences with more rhythm
- Pushed off of his hocks, with more drive over his fences
- Was more rounded in its spine and thus had more symmetry in its jumps
- Took more appropriate strides between fences
- Was more balanced in its jumps
- Had more confidence over fences and in its stride
- Was softer in its landing
- Was more controlled over the fences
- Had more lift to its shoulders over both jumps
- Jumped with more desirable form and proper momentum
- Showed less hesitation prior to takeoffs at each fence
- Looked through the bridle with more expression over the fences
- More correctly rated the fences
- Was faulted for a rub (tick of the rail)
- Was faulted for rapping the fence (hitting of the rail)
- Was cleaner over the fences

SAMPLE REASONS: HUNTER HACK

Sir,

I liked this class of hunter hack horses 1-2-3-4. I started with 1, the bay, as he was the most correct in his combination of jumping ability, brokeness, and quality of motion. In relation to 2, he was more direct in his approach, jumping more evenly off both hind legs with a rounder form and more arc to his spine. He duplicated this performance on his second fence, following which he had a smoother lead change and extended his stride more in the hand-gallop. He was more relaxed in the halt, displaying a greater ability to relax and recover when the rider dropped the reins.

Moving to my intermediate pair of individuals, who both jumped early for their second fence, I used 2 over 3 because 2 exhibited more self-carriage. He was more correctly hinged in his shoulder and hip; consequently, he was flatter and more forward off his forehand and lifted his back more, thus enabling him to strike off into the canter with a deeper hock. He was more preferred in his frame and moved with a softer foot to ground contact.

Dropping to my final pair, it was 3 over 4, as 3 was more relaxed in his courtesy circle; stayed more evenly between the reins, and was more correct down the line, as he did not change leads. Yes, 4 was a flatter-kneed, longer-striding individual; however, 3 placed his jumps more near to center between the standards.

Today, 4, the gray, was my bottom, as he lacked brokeness, was inconsistent in his approaches, and swapped leads prior to his second fence. Furthermore, he was against the bridle and negative in his expression during his hand-gallop. He ran through the bridle when asked to stop and was resistant while backing. Thank you.

HUNTER UNDER SADDLE

AQHA HANDBOOK, 2025

Hunters under saddle should be suitable to purpose. They should be obedient, alert, and responsive to their riders. They should move in a long, low frame and be able to lengthen their stride and cover ground, as in traveling over hunt country following hounds. Horses should be serviceably sound, and quick, short strides should be penalized. Judges should emphasize free movement and manners. Horses are to be shown at a walk, a trot, and a canter both ways of the ring. Horses should back easily and stand quietly. Light contact with the horse's mouth is recommended.

At the option of the judge, all or just the top eight horses may be required to hand-gallop one or both ways of the ring. Never more than eight horses are to hand-gallop at one time. At the hand-gallop, the judge may ask the group to halt and stand quietly on a free (loosened) rein.

The walk should be forward, rhythmical, and flat-footed. An extremely slow walk is to be penalized. The trot should be long, low, ground-covering, cadenced, and balanced. Smoothness is more essential than speed. Extreme speed is to be penalized, as is excessive knee action. The canter should be smooth, free-moving, relaxed, and straight on both leads. The stride should be suitable to cover ground following hounds. An overcollected four-beat canter is to be penalized, as is excessive speed. The hand-gallop should show a definite lengthening of stride with a noticeable difference in speed. The horse should be under control at all times and should be able to pull up (not a sliding stop) and stand quietly.

HUNTER UNDER SADDLE TERMS

- Moved out with a bolder, more determined stride
- Moved out with a lower frame
- Was flatter-footed, more relaxed at the walk
- Was more cadenced at the trot
- Had more hindquarter impulsion
- Was lighter on the forehand
- Slipped across the ground lower and leveler, showing greater reach of forearm at the walk, trot, and canter
- Was more correct in the placement of face and poll
- Showed more expression while working
- Was lower, flatter, and smoother-moving

Follow QR code for example of desirable performance of trot and canter for stock type Hunter Under Saddle (https://docs.lib.purdue.edu/horseevaluation/1)

- Maintained frame into all transitions
- Was more responsive to the rider, picking up both leads quickly and more correctly and going both ways in a quieter fashion
- Was more forward into the trot with more hindquarter impulsion
- Was more extended and freer-moving
- Was a flashier mover who sets itself apart from the rest
- Had more pure cadence
- Had more elasticity, hinge, and swing from shoulders and hips
- Engaged its hindquarter with more drive and impulsion
- Showed more energy and purpose of stride at the trot
- Had a longer, flatter, more reaching stride
- Showed more cadence of stride
- Showed more forward impulsion
- Was more suitable to purpose
- Had a more pleasing hunter form
- Showed more flow to its stride
- Was bolder-trotting
- Showed more impulsion and drive off its hocks
- Was a bolder-moving horse that showed more length of stride as well as more impulsion and drive off its socks
- Exhibited greater forward impulsion from the hindquarters while at the canter
- Showed more shoulder and stifle freedom
- Moved in a more correct Hunter Under Saddle frame
- Was flatter, more forward at the trot
- Was a slower-legged, longer-striding individual who was softer in foot-to-ground contact
- Had a longer, more even stride
- Was softer in its poll and more supple in its neck
- Moved with a lower center of gravity
- Covered more ground with fewer strides
- Was a more supple, freer-striding individual who exhibited more forward motion

- Displayed more fluidity and smoothness at both the trot and the canter
- Had a more ground-covering stride without quickening its gait
- Had a more floating trot with a flatter knee and more point from knee to toe
- Had more flexion through the poll, allowing the horse to be flatter and more forward in its movement
- Had more reach to his stride
- Was more correctly hinged in his shoulder and hip, and consequently the horse lifted it back more, thus enabling it to strike off into the canter with more reach and point off the forehand and a deeper hock behind

SAMPLE REASONS: HUNTER UNDER SADDLE

I liked the Hunter Under Saddle 4-1-3-2. I started today with 4, the sorrel, as he was the most correct in his combination of Hunter Under Saddle type and quality of motion. In relation to 1, 4 was a more broke, consistent, and collected individual who had a truer cadence and rhythm at all three gaits. He stayed more evenly between the reins, requiring less adjustment from the rider. He was smoother in his transitions, being more accepting of the rider's cues when asked to canter to the right.

Additionally, he gave more to the bridle when asked to back.

Moving to my intermediate pair, I used 1 over 3, as she was a more connected horse who exhibited more self-carriage. She was more correctly hinged in her shoulder and hip; consequently, lifting her back more enabled her to strike off into the canter with more reach off her forehand and a deeper step behind. Yes, 3 was handled less throughout the class, but this does not change the fact that 1 is a longer-striding horse who has more Hunter Under Saddle type.

Dropping to my final pair, it's 3, the flea-bitten gray, over 2, with the major focus on brokeness. 3 was smoother in his transitions from trot to walk working to the left, as he did not require schooling. There is no question that 2 is a flatter-kneed, longer-striding individual. However, 3 was still freer from major faults and gave a more honest and steady ride.

Today, 2, the dark gray, is my bottom, as he was handled heavily following the trot while working to the left. This resulted in him being on-the-muscle and high-headed and requiring schooling for the rest of the class. Thank you.

PLANTATION PLEASURE

Plantation Pleasure is a class in the Tennessee Walking Horse performance division. The horses are judged on quality of movement and manners. The flat walk and the famed running walk are both a basic, loose, four-cornered gait, a 1-2-3-4 beat with each of the horse's feet hitting the ground separately at regular intervals. As the horse moves, its head will nod in rhythm with the regular rise and fall of its hooves, overstriding the track left by its front foot with its hind foot. In general, the horse should travel in a straight, direct motion, never winging, crossing, or swinging. The flat walk should be loose, bold, and square with plenty of shoulder motion. The running walk should also be executed with loose ease of movement, pulling with the forefeet and pushing and driving with the hind feet. There should be a noticeable difference in the rate of speed between the flat walk and the running walk. A good running walk should never allow proper form to be sacrificed for excessive speed. Judging should be influenced not by speed but instead by true form exhibited. Credit should be given to horses that maintain form and perform with brilliance and animation.

The rocking-chair canter is a high, rolling gait with distinct head movement and with the chin tucked and in a smooth and collected movement. The horse must be straight and true on both leads.

PLANTATION PLEASURE TERMS

- Exhibited more rolling motion from the shoulder
- Had more drive from behind allowing, the horse more reach from the hindquarters
- Showed more brilliance and animation in its movement
- Had a bolder-strided running walk
- Exhibited a bolder, squarer flat walk
- Combined show-ring presence, manner, and responsiveness to a higher degree
- Showed more front-end elevation, drive, and impulsion from behind, allowing for a more rolling canter
- Had a smoother, more rolling canter
- Was more effortless in its transitions
- Wore the bridle with more pride and elegance
- Was more vertical about the face
- Was prouder in its head and tail carriage
- Was a more up-headed individual
- Showed more ring presence and attitude
- Broke over higher in its knees
- Exhibited higher, rounder motion

PLANTATION PLEASURE REASONS

Sir,

I placed the Plantation Pleasure class 1-2-3-4, finding my top pair of horses to be bolder and more animated movers and the bottom pair exhibiting less consistency of manners.

In my top pair, I placed the chestnut, 1, over the gray, 2, as 1 displayed more of an elastic and bold flat walk and had a stronger, more animated running walk that exhibited more overstride. 1 also showed more response to his rider's aids and cues. I realize that 2 exhibited a more rolling and smooth rocking-chair canter; however, it was still the sorrel, 1, that showed more elasticity of stride and better overall manners.

In my middle pair, I placed the gray, 2, over the bay, 3, feeling that 2 was smoother and more effortless in his transitions and performed with a more mannerly and interested attitude. I will grant that 3 showed more overstride and head nod, but it was still the gray 2 that had the more ideal disposition and consistency of gait.

Moving on to my bottom pair, I placed the bay, 3, over the chestnut 4, as 3 showed higher, rounder motion in her front legs and required less contact to her mouth. I can appreciate that 4 had a more ground-covering walk; however, it was 3 that showed more balance and presence.

Even though he showed a great deal of drive and impulsion off of his hocks, I placed the chestnut, 4, on the bottom because he was rough in his transitions, missed his right lead, refused to back, and lacked the overall presence, manners, and quality of movement to be placed any higher in the class today. Thank you!

PLEASURE DRIVING

The stock-type pleasure driving class strives for the same quality of movement exhibited in the Hunter Under Saddle class. The walk should have an average, flat-footed, relaxed stride. The park gait should be a long yet easy-strided working trot. An obvious change of speed is to be made into the road gait, which is a faster gait with a more extended and reaching stride. There is a backup in this class. Ideally, there should be a powerful and effortless stride.

Pleasure driving in breeds such as Morgans, Saddlebreds, and Arabians call for more animation and vertical movement in the gaits, similar to their respective English Pleasure and Three-Gaited classes. In these breeds, a more up-headed individual, breaking over higher in the knees and showing more ring presence and breed type, is the ideal.

PLEASURE DRIVING TERMS

- Worked straighter through the shafts
- Showed more change of speed from . . .
- Moved out with more eagerness and impulsion into the road gait
- Was more suitable in its work, as the horse stood quieter, backed more readily, and worked in a more relaxed and cooperative manner down the rail
- Was steadier and more responsive in the reverse
- Turned with more smoothness and efficiency in the corners
- Stopped with more control

SAMPLE REASONS: PLEASURE DRIVING

Quality of movement and manners were the criteria I used in placing the pleasure driving 3-4-1-2. I had an obvious top pair, starting with the sorrel horse that combined impulsion and fluency to a higher degree. I put the black horse on bottom, as he moved asymmetrically from his shoulder and bobbed his head.

In my top pair, I put 3, the long-strided sorrel, over 4, the gray, as 3 showed more energy and determination to a road gait that had less speed and more length to each stride. 3 showed more change of speed from the park to the road gait, was more supple in the poll, and was comparatively more horizontal across the neck. Furthermore, he was more elevated in the shoulders and had more lift and strength across the back, allowing for a more effortless way of going. I can appreciate that 4 was smoother in the transition down to the walk and used his shoulders more efficiently in the reverse; however, it was 3 that traveled in a longer, lower hunter frame, combining hindquarter impulsion and style to a higher degree.

For my middle pair, I easily had the gray, 4, over the bay, 1, since it was 4 that gave a better-mannered performance, as he was quieter in the mouth and tail, showed less resistance in the face, and worked straighter through the shafts. 4 was also more consistent in speed and frame. I realize that 1 had the ability to move out in the road gait with more drive from behind and less weight in the front, giving him a longer, flatter-kneed stride, but it was 4 that maintained a consistent way of going, showing more eagerness to work and willingness to respond.

For my final pair, it was 1, the even-strided bay, over 2, the black, since 1 exhibited a more two-beat diagonal road and park gait, working with more symmetry from the shoulders, allowing him to maintain a steadier, more consistent head carriage. I grant that 2 did give a quieter, more relaxed performance and required less prompting for the backup; however, it was 1 that used the proper rhythm and cadence in the trot and showed less duress throughout each gait. The fact that 2 gave a quiet, well-mannered performance could not compensate for the fact that he was short-strided in his front left and bobbed his head. His lack of cadence, collection, and quality of movement could simply merit him no higher placing today. Thank you!

RANCH RIDING

AQHA HANDBOOK, 2025

The purpose of the ranch riding class is to measure the ability of the horse to be a pleasure to ride while being used as a means of conveyance from performing one ranch task to another. The horse should reflect the versatility, attitude, and movement of a working ranch horse riding outside the confines of an arena. The horse should be well trained, relaxed, quiet, and soft and cadenced at all gaits. The ideal ranch horse will travel with forward movement and demonstrate an obvious lengthening of stride at extended gaits. The horse can be ridden with light contact or on a relatively loose rein without requiring undue restraint but should not be shown on a full drape of reins. The overall manners and responsiveness of the ranch riding horse to make timely transitions in a smooth and correct manner as well as the quality of the movement are primary considerations. The ideal ranch riding horse should have a natural ranch horse appearance from head to tail in each maneuver.

Horses will be worked through a pattern individually and will be scored from 0 to 100, with 70 indicating an average score. Each maneuver is scored individually (-1 1/2 extremely poor, -1 very poor, -1/2 poor, 0 correct, +1/2 good, +1 very good, +1 1/2 excellent). Penalties are scored independently of maneuver scores. An overall score from -1 1/2 to +1 1/2 should also be given for overall natural ranch horse appearance.

Note: The ranch division is one of the fastest-growing divisions in all of horse showing, in multiple breeds. Different breeds and associations may call classes slightly different things. Check the rule book governing the contest to ensure you are judging the correct ranch class.

Faults to be scored according to severity:

1. Opening/gapping mouth excessively
2. Stumbling
3. Use of spur in front of the cinch
4. If horse appears sullen, dull, lethargic, emaciated, drawn, or overly tired
5. Quick, choppy, or pony-strided
6. Overly canted at the lope (horses that lope with haunches in toward the center of arena)
7. Excessive head bobbing
8. Excessive ringing of tail

Credits:

1. Natural ground-covering gaits
2. Consistency at all gaits
3. Smooth upward and downward transitions
4. Works on reasonably loose rein without excessive cueing to maintain moderate pace

5. Giving the appearance of being able to do a day's work
6. Athletic ability/agile
7. Softness of horses' chin, poll, neck, shoulder, body, and hip and being broke through the whole body

Penalties:

1-Point Penalties:

- Too slow (per gait)
- Overbridled (per maneuver)
- Out of frame (per maneuver)
- Break of gait at walk or trot for two strides or less
- Wrong lead or out of lead for two strides or less

3-Point Penalties:

- Break of gait at walk or trot for more than two strides
- Break of gait at lope except when correcting an incorrect lead
- Wrong lead or out of lead
- Draped reins (per maneuver)
- Out of lead or cross-cantering more than two strides when changing leads
- Trotting more than three strides when making a simple lead change
- Trotting for more than three strides in lope departures or exiting a rollback into a lope from a stop or walk
- Severe disturbance of any obstacle

5-Point Penalties:

- Blatant disobedience (kick, bite, buck, rear, etc.) for each refusal

Off pattern, placed below horses performing all maneuvers:

- Eliminates or adds maneuver
- Incomplete maneuver
- Repeated blatant disobedience
- Use of two hands (except junior and level 1 horses shown in a snaffle bit/hackamore), more than one finger between split reins or any fingers between romal reins (except in the two rein)

Zero (0) score:

- Illegal equipment including hoof black, braided or banded manes, and tail extensions
- Abuse
- Leaving the working area before the pattern is complete
- Lameness
- Disrespect or misconduct

- Improper western attire
- Fall of horse/rider

Follow QR code for video example of ideal ranch riding horse from the American Paint Horse Association (https://docs.lib.purdue.edu/horseevaluation/2)

RANCH RIDING TERMS

- Walk
- Jog
- Lope
- Required less handling
- Had a softer foot-to-ground contact
- Moved forward in all three gaits
- Had a more ground-covering stride
- Required less checking on the part of the rider
- Was smoother in its upward and downward transitions

SAMPLE REASONS: RANCH RIDING

I placed the ranch riding 1-2-3-4.

In a more pattern-precise top pair, it was 1's ranch horse utility that places him over 2. The bay walked with more purpose, and reached out with a longer, more ground-consuming stride when asked to extend at both the jog and the lope. Furthermore, he turned more willingly around a more stationary pivot foot. Now, I won't argue that 2 was more level from poll to wither, but he falls to second place when he receives a one-point penalty for being too slow at the extended lope.

Even so, it's 2's workmanlike attitude that places him over 3. The dapple gray was more responsive to the rider's aids and cues, requiring less obvious guidance especially in the transitions. Sure, 3 covered more ground at all gaits, but this could not compensate for the fact that he was extremely resistant throughout the pattern, causing him to be late in the first downward transition to the jog.

In an ill-mannered final pair, it comes down to penalty points to sort 3 over 4. Not only was the black more precise in the placement of his simple lead change, but he also navigated the walk logs with more accuracy. Sure, 4 was more willfully guided at times, but he finds his home at the bottom when he takes more than three strides to perform a simple lead change and severely disturbs the walk logs for two three-point penalties. Thank you.

REINING

NRHA HANDBOOK, 2025

In reining, each contestant performs the required pattern individually and separately. "To rein a horse is not only to guide him, but to also control his every move. The best reined horse should be willfully guided or controlled with little or no apparent resistance and dictated to completely." Credit will be given for smoothness, finesse, attitude, quickness, and authority in performing the various maneuvers while using controlled speed. Each individual performance is scored on a basis of 0 to infinity, with 70 denoting an average performance.

SCORING GUIDELINES

Reining is scored using a combination of maneuver scores, which give a score to each movement of the pattern, and penalty scoring, which gives a standardized penalty for specific infractions.

Maneuver scoring: Points will be added or subtracted from the eight maneuvers in the pattern on the following basis. These will be indicated in the maneuver scores space on the reining score sheet and are independent of the penalty points.

+1 1/2 excellent
+1 very good
+1/2 good
0 average (maneuver performed correctly but with no degree of difficulty)
−1/2 poor
−1 very poor
−1 1/2 extremely poor

PENALTY SCORING

Penalty scores are indicated in the penalty score box on the reining score sheet. Reining has the following standardized penalties:

No score: (Cannot place in a reining competition, but you must place in a judging contest)

- Abuse of the animal
- Use of illegal equipment
- Use of illegal bits, bosals, or curb chains
- Use of tack collars, tie downs, or nose bands
- Use of whips or bats
- Use of any attachment that may alter the movement of or circulation to the tail
- Failure to provide horse and equipment to the appropriate judge for inspection
- Disrespect or misconduct by the exhibitor
- Closed reins are not allowed except as standard romal reins and mecates on bosals in classes, where the use of two hands is allowed.
- Excess rein may be straightened anytime during the pattern, provided the rider's free hand remains behind the rein hand. Any attempt to alter tension or length of the reins from bridle to the rein hand is to be considered

use of two hands, and a penalty score of zero will be applied. In addition, should the judge determine that the free hand is being used to instill fear or praise, a penalty of 5 will be applied as well as a reduction in the maneuver score.

Zero (0) score: (Can place in a reining competition and should place above a no score in a judging contest)

- Use of more than the index or first finger between the reins
- Use of two hands or changing hands (except with snaffle bit or hackamore)
- Use of romal other than as approved by NRHA regulations
- Failure to complete the pattern as written
- Performing the maneuvers other than in specified order
- The inclusion of maneuvers not specified, including, but not limited to
    - Backing more than two strides
    - Turning more than 90 degrees
    - On run-in patterns, once beginning a lope, a complete stop prior to reaching the first marker. (Exception: a complete stop in the first quarter of a circle after a lope departure is not to be considered an inclusion of maneuver; a two-point break of gait penalty will apply.)
    - Equipment failure that delays completion of pattern
    - Balking or refusal of command where pattern is delayed
    - Running away or failing to guide where it becomes impossible to discern whether the entry is off-pattern
    - Jogging in excess of half a circle or half the length of the arena
    - Overspins of more than a one-quarter turn
- Fall to the ground by horse or rider
- When going to and coming out of a rollback in a pattern requiring a run-around, a rollback that crosses the center line
- Failure to wear appropriate western attire as outlined by NRHA handbook (in most judging contests, tack and attire are considered legal, and this would not be a penalty)

Five-point point penalties:

- Holding saddle with free hand
- Spurring in front of the cinch
- Use of free hand to instill fear or praise
- Blatant disobediences including kicking, biting, bucking, rearing, and striking
- Horse dropping to its knees or hocks

Two-point penalties:

- Break of gait
- Freezing up in spins or rollback
- On walk-in patterns, loping prior to reaching the center of the arena and/or failure to stop or walk before executing a lope departure
- On run-in patterns, failure to be in a lope prior to first marker or break of gait prior to the first marker

- Horse does not completely pass the specified marker before initiating a stop position
- Jogging beyond two strides but less than half a circle or half the length of the arena
- In patterns requiring a run-around, failure to be on the correct lead when round the end of the arena for more than half of the turn

One-point penalties:

- Over- or underspinning one-eighth to one-fourth turn
- In patterns requiring a run-around; failure to be on the correct lead when rounding the end of the arena for half of the turn or less
- Each time a horse is out of lead, a judge is required to deduct one point. This is a cumulative penalty, and the judge will add one point for each one-quarterf the circumference of a circle or any part thereof that a horse is out of lead.

Half-point penalty:

- Delayed change of lead by one stride
- Starting a circle at a jog or exiting a rollback at a jog up to two strides
- In patterns requiring a run-around, failure to be on the correct lead when rounding the end of the arena for half of the turn or less
- Over- or underspinning up to one-eighth of a turn
- Failure to remain a minimum of twenty feet from the wall or fence when approaching a stop and/or a rollback
- Severely stumbles, significantly detracting from the maneuver
- Faults against the horse (to be scored accordingly but not to cause disqualification):
  - Opening mouth excessively (when wearing a bit)
  - Excessive jawing, open mouth, or head-raising in stops
  - Lacking a smooth, straight stop on haunches
  - Refusing to change leads
  - Anticipating signals
  - Stumbling or falling
  - Backing sideways
  - Knocking over markers

REINING TERMS

- Ran harder, slid farther while melting its hocks deeper and straighter into the ground, staying quieter in the mouth and more relaxed off the forehand while stopping
- Was a more athletic individual who ran its pattern with more speed and dispatch
- Held a more stationary pivot foot during its faster, flatter spins
- Smoother-circling individual who stayed more upright in the shoulder
- Was more preferred in the size and shape of its circles, as they met more near to the center during the more simultaneous lead changes
- Rolled back harder and crisper over its hocks

- Showed less anticipation of stops, and thus was freer from scotching
- Stayed more relaxed and supple down the spine, allowing the horse to stop harder and slide farther while staying more mobile off its forehand
- Held a lower center of gravity during the faster, more accurate spins
- Was more controlled in its stops and slides
- Was relaxed and more workmanlike in its execution of the maneuvers
- Ran a more demanding pattern with a more appropriate use of speed
- Ran with a higher degree of confidence into its rundowns
- Ran the faster pattern
- Was more exact in the execution of its spins
- Was more sure-footed in its circles
- Was more functionally correct
- Maintained a more stationary pivot while providing more reach and extension from the inside front and crossing more cleanly from the outside front
- Had more balance to its spins
- Had a truer, more athletic pattern
- Showed more speed
- Showed more precision
- Showed more control
- Was cooler, calmer, and more collected
- Contrasted large, fast with small, slow
- More aggressively executed the pattern (or a maneuver)
- Acquired fewer penalties
- Was crisp and exact in lead changes
- Required less reining in the determination of its circles
- Had more impulsion in rundowns
- Was speedier and more aggressive in its rundowns, reaching more extensively with the forearm while maintaining a lower, rounder frame into its stops
- Showed more speed variation
- Ran the faster pattern with more control and authority
- Showed more willingness and precision in executing the prescribed pattern
- Showed more pattern preciseness
- Accomplished more in its pattern
- Simply got more done
- Was harder-stopping, faster-turning, smoother-circling, and longer-sliding
- Was more fundamentally correct throughout the pattern
- Ran a more difficult and demanding pattern and yet showed a more positive attitude
- Rider had a greater degree of handle on the horse, thus requiring less excessive reining and leg cues
- Showed more finesse and quickness in the pattern
- Exhibited a more complete picture of control, smoothness, and speed
- Was less restricted in all parts of the pattern
- Ran the pattern more accurately and with more effort and control from horse and rider

- Stayed more upright in its shoulders throughout the pattern
- Had more pattern desirability throughout
- Overpowered the class with athletic ability
- Dropped deeper into the ground with its hindquarters and remained more mobile in front
- Had more controlled stops
- Dropped deeper into the ground
- Dropped its hocks deeper into the ground
- Stopped with its haunches deeper in the ground
- Had more stylish stops, being deeper and longer
- Deeper, straighter slides
- Had longer slides
- Was more pleasing in its stops, maintaining more desirable hindquarter positioning, staying flatter in front, and being less elevated in its poll and shoulders
- Was a smoother, longer-stopping horse
- Stopped squarer
- Worked more off its haunches and maintained movement in its front end, allowing the horse to have a more relaxed stop
- Dropped its hindquarters deeper into the ground while keeping the front legs relaxed, allowing the horse to execute a more correct sliding stop
- Stopped harder in a straighter, longer, and more correct track
- Was a smoother-stopping horse that stayed more relaxed and supple down its spine, thus allowing the horse to slide farther
- Was more preferred in the frame during its stops, being more rounded in the spine, thus enabling the horse to drive its hocks deeper into the ground and stay more relaxed on its forehand
- Remained more mobile in front
- Was freer from blocking on its forehand
- Drove out harder in the runs, stopped smoother, and slid farther
- Ran with greater speed and dispatch from end to end, rolling back cleaner over its hocks
- Ran harder with less hesitation into its stops
- Ran with more authority and aggressiveness into its stops
- Ran harder with less anticipation in the straightaway
- Was freer from blasting during its runs
- Showed more uniformity to the size of its circles
- Showed more size and speed variation in its circles
- Was more desirable in shoulder usage in its circles
- Performed its circles in a more correct and precise manner
- Dropped back more obediently into the slow circles, holding its body more correctly while keeping a more steady pace
- Was more correct in the size, speed, and symmetry of its circles
- Was more correct in its hind leg follow-up
- Ran flatter and smoother circles, staying lighter and more responsive between the reins
- Exhibited greater contrast in the speed and size of the circles

JUDGING PERFORMANCE / 59

- Showed greater control of the arena ground by staying more within the markers while displaying smoother and more balanced circles
- Was softer in the bridle, following a lighter rein in its more precisely executed circles
- Ran the figure eights with more speed and was more fluid in the lead changes
- Was more balanced in the figure eights, opening its stride without hesitation in the fast circles while slowing down more promptly into more evenly shaped small circles
- Ran a more symmetrical figure eight
- Was more prompt and exact in its lead changes
- Was more proficient in its lead changes, stops, and turns
- Was flatter in its lead changes
- Was flatter and more forward in its transitions
- Had more balanced spins
- Had faster spins while remaining flat, holding a more stationary pivot foot
- Had greater sharpness to its spins, turning more ideally over its haunches while maintaining a lower center of gravity
- Had a tighter hock during its spins
- Had flatter, more consistent spins
- Had smoother, flatter spins
- Was more correct about body alignment in its spins
- Rolled back more over its haunches
- Performed its rollbacks in a more correct and willing manner
- Performed more correct rollbacks, with them being more over its haunches
- Rolled over the hocks more correctly with a more stationary pivot foot
- Rolled back cleaner over the hocks
- Rolled back harder over the hocks
- Worked over its hock more correctly, as it rolled back harder and crisper
- Showed more finesse to its pivots
- Performed its pivots with more confidence and ease
- Pivoted over its inside leg more correctly
- Backed more readily over its tracks
- Had a faster, straighter back and settled more readily
- Lowered its head, tucked its nose, and backed straighter and squarer over the hocks
- Flexed it poll, relaxed its jaw, and backed in a straighter fashion
- Was a faster, straighter-backing horse
- Worked more efficiently and with a more cooperative attitude
- Was a more willing worker that performed in a more positive manner
- More readily yielded to its rider's cues
- Performed with greater willingness
- Was quieter about the mouth and the tail

SAMPLE REASONS: REINING I

I liked the reining 2-4-3-1. I started with 2, the bay, as he was the most correct in his combination of reining talent and athletic ability. In relation to 4, 2 exhibited more control while running his more symmetrical circles. He held a more stationary pivot foot and was more precise in the placement of his faster spins. Yes, 4 ran harder while circling. However, 2 showed less anticipation of the riders cues, staying more evenly between the reins and requiring less handling.

Moving to my intermediate pair, it is 4, the black, over 3, as 4 was a more athletic individual who ran his circles with more aggression. He dropped his hindquarters deeper into the ground, flexing his loin more, and thus had a longer, deeper sliding stop. I realize that 3 backed with less resistance, and I will admit that both horses had lead-changing problems. Even still, 4 rolled back crisper over his hocks with a more prompt lope-off.

Dropping to my final pair, I used 3, the Paint, over 1 simply because 3 performed the correct number of spins in both directions. There is no doubt that 1 ran his circles with more aggression and was flatter and faster in his spins, exhibiting more reining talent. But this does not change the fact that 3 had a more problem-free performance.

Today 1, the sorrel, is my bottom. I faulted him and placed him fourth, as he overspun by a full revolution for a score of zero. Thank you.

SAMPLE REASONS: REINING II
I placed the reining 4-1-2-3. I started with 4, the sorrel, as he was the most correct in his combination of athletic ability and pattern precision. In relation to 1, 4 worked a more difficult and demanding pattern, as he ran harder and slid farther, melting his hocks deeper and straighter into the ground while staying more relaxed and mobile off his forehand, following which he rolled back crisper and harder over his hocks. He demonstrated greater sharpness to his spins, turning more ideally over his haunches, staying flatter, and holding a more stationary pivot foot.

Moving to my intermediate placing, it is 1 over 2, as 1 ran his circles with more aggression and variation in speed, staying more upright in his shoulder and more even between the reins with smoother and more precise lead changes. Yes, 2 was freer from overspinning. However, 1 held a lower center of gravity during his faster, flatter spins.

Dropping to my final pair, I used 2 over 3, as 2 had a more fundamentally correct pattern, as he did not add a spin. Furthermore, he was lighter in the rider's hands, staying more in the bridle when asked to stop. He simply exhibited more pattern precision.

Today 3, the sorrel, is my bottom. I faulted him and placed him fourth, as he was the high-headed horse that came out of the bridle when asked to stop, was against the rein, and dropped his shoulders while circling, not to mention that he received a total of three penalty points for being out of lead for three quadrants of his final circle. Thank you.

SHOWMANSHIP

AQHA HANDBOOK, 2025

Showmanship is designed to evaluate the exhibitor's ability to execute, in concert with a well-groomed and conditioned horse, a set of maneuvers prescribed by the judge with precision and smoothness while exhibiting poise and confidence and maintaining a balanced, functional, and fundamentally correct body position.

OVERALL PRESENTATION OF EXHIBITOR AND HORSE
The exhibitor's overall poise, confidence, appearance, and position throughout the class and the physical appearance of the horse will be evaluated. Exhibitors should be poised, confident, courteous, and genuinely

sportsmanlike at all times, quickly recognizing and correcting faults in the positioning of the horse. The exhibitor should continue showing the horse until the class has been placed or has been excused unless otherwise instructed by the judge. The exhibitor should appear businesslike, stand and move in a straight, have a natural and upright manner, and avoid excessive, unnatural, or animated body positions.

The exhibitor must lead on the horse's left side while holding the lead shank in the right hand near the halter, with the tail of the lead loosely coiled in the left hand unless requested by the judge to show the horse's teeth. It is preferable that the exhibitor's hand not be on the snap or chain portion of the lead continuously. The excess lead should never be tightly coiled, rolled, or folded. When leading, the exhibitor should be positioned between the eye and the midpoint of the horse's neck, referred to as the leading position.

Both arms should be bent at the elbow, with the elbows held close to the exhibitor's side and the forearms held in a natural position. Height of the arms may vary depending on the size of the horse and the exhibitor, but the arms should never be held straight out with the elbows locked.

The position of the exhibitor when executing a turn to the right is the same as the leading position except that the exhibitor should turn and face toward the horse's head and have the horse move away from the exhibitor to the right.

When executing a back, the exhibitor should turn from the leading position to face toward the rear of the horse, with the right hand extended in front of the exhibitor's chest and still maintaining a slight bend in the elbow, and walk forward. The ideal position is for the exhibitor's left shoulder to be in alignment with the horse's left front leg.

When setting the horse up for inspection, the exhibitor should stand angled toward the horse in a position between the horse's eye and muzzle and should never leave the head of the horse. The exhibitor is required to use the quarter method when presenting the horse. Exhibitors should maintain a position that is safe for themselves and the judge. The position of the exhibitor should not obstruct the judge's view of the horse and should allow the exhibitor to maintain awareness of the judge's position at all times. The exhibitor should not crowd other exhibitors when setting up side by side or head to tail. When moving around the horse, the exhibitor should change sides in front of the horse with minimal steps and should assume the same position on the right side of the horse that the exhibitor had on the left side.

Leading, backing, turning, and initiating the setup should be performed from the left side of the horse. At no time should the exhibitor stand directly in front of the horse. The exhibitor should not touch the horse with their hands or feet or visibly cue the horse by pointing their feet at the horse during the setup.

Presentation of horse. The horse's body condition and overall fitness should be assessed. The hair coat should be clean, well brushed, and in good condition. The mane, tail, forelock, and wither tuft may not contain ornaments (ribbons, bows, etc.) but may be braided or banded for English or Western.

Scoring. Exhibitors are to be scored from 0 to infinity, with 70 denoting an average performance. Patterns will be divided into six to ten maneuvers, as specified by the judge, and each maneuver will be scored from +3 to -3, with 1/2-point increments acceptable that will be added or subtracted from 70.

Maneuver scores should be determined independent of penalties and should reflect equal consideration of both the performance of the exhibitor's pattern and the form and effectiveness of the exhibitor and presentation of horse, to result in the following scores: +3 excellent, +2 very good, +1 good, 0 average or correct, -1 poor, -2 very poor, -3 extremely poor. Exhibitors overall form and effectiveness should also be scored from 0 to 5 with 0 to 2 average, 3 good, 4 very good, and 5 excellent.

Pattern performance. The exhibitor should perform the work accurately, precisely, and smoothly and with a reasonable amount of speed. Increasing speed of the work increases the degree of difficulty; however, accuracy and precision should not be sacrificed for speed. The horse should lead, stop, back, turn, and set up willingly, briskly, and readily with minimal visible or audible cueing. Severe disobedience will not result in a disqualification but should be penalized severely, and the exhibitor should not place above an exhibitor who completes the pattern correctly. Excessive schooling or training, willful abuse, loss of control of the horse by the exhibitor, failure to follow the prescribed pattern, and knocking over or working on the wrong side of the cones shall be cause for disqualification.

The horse should be led directly to and away from the judge in a straight or curved line and track briskly and freely at the prescribed gait as instructed. The horse's head and neck should be straight and in line with the body. The stop should be straight, prompt, smooth, and responsive, with the horse's body remaining straight. The horse should back up readily, with the head, neck, and body aligned in a straight or curved line as instructed.

On turns of greater than 90 degrees, the ideal turn consists of the horse pivoting on the right hind leg while stepping across and in front of the right front leg with the left front leg. An exhibitor should not be penalized if the horse performs a pivot on the left hind leg, but an exhibitor whose horse performs the pivot correctly should receive more credit. A pull turn to the left is an unacceptable maneuver.

The horse should be set up quickly, with the feet squarely underneath the body.

The exhibitor does not have to reset a horse that stops square.

An exhibitor should be penalized in the pattern independent of maneuver scores and deducted from the final score as follows:

Three Points
    Break of gait at the walk or trot up to two strides
    Over- or underturning up to one-eighth of a turn
    Ticking or hitting a cone
    Sliding a pivot foot
    Lifting a pivot foot during a pivot or setup and replacing it in the same place
    Lifting a foot in a setup and replacing it in the same place after presentation

Five Points
    Not performing the specific gait or not stopping within ten feet (three meters) of the designated location
    Break of gait at walk or trot for more than two strides
    Splitting the cone (cone between the horse and the exhibitor)
    Horse stepping out of or moving the hind end significantly during a pivot or turn
    Horse stepping out of setup after presentation
    Horse resting a foot or hipshot in a setup
    Over- or underturning one-eighth to one-quarter of a turn

Ten Points
    Exhibitor is not in the required position during inspection

Exhibitor touching the horse or kicking or pointing their feet at the horse's feet during the setup

Standing directly in front of the horse

Loss of lead shank, holding chain or two hands on shank

Blatant disobedience including kicking, rearing, or pawing; horse continually circling exhibitor

Horse stepping out of or moving the hind end significantly during a pivot or turn more than one time

Disqualifications: Remember to keep judging. Unlike in a horse show, in a judging contest you must place every one of the four horses, and if more than one horse disqualifies, you need to be able to differentiate between them.

Loss of control of horse that endangers exhibitor, other horses, or the judge

Horse becomes separated from the exhibitor

Failure to display the correct number

Willful abuse

Excessive schooling or training; use of artificial aids

Illegal equipment

Off pattern, including knocking over or being on the wrong side of a cone or marker; never performing the designated gait; over- or underturning more than one-quarter of a turn

Example of completed showmanship score sheet

Follow QR code for video example of excellent showmanship run (https://docs.lib.purdue.edu/horseevaluation/5)

TRAIL

AQHA HANDBOOK, 2025

This class will be judged on the performance of the horse over obstacles, with emphasis on manners, response to the rider, and quality of movement. Credit will be given to horses negotiating the obstacles with style and some degree of speed, providing that correctness is not sacrificed. Horses should receive credit for showing attentiveness to the obstacles and the capability of picking their own way through the course when obstacles warrant it and willingly responding to the rider's cues on more difficult obstacles. Horses shall be penalized for any unnecessary delay while approaching or negotiating the obstacles.

SCORING FOR TRAIL

Scoring will be on the basis of 0 to infinity, with 70 denoting an average performance. Each obstacle will receive an obstacle score that should be added or subtracted from 70 and is subject to a penalty that should be subtracted. Trail is scored using a combination of obstacle scores (similar to maneuver scores in reining and western riding) and penalty scores.

OBSTACLE SCORING

Each obstacle will be scored and assessed independently of penalty scores. The obstacle score indicates how well the horse and rider performed on each component of the trail course. Scoring is done on the following basis:

+1 1/2 excellent
+1 very good
+1/2 good
0 average (maneuver performed correctly but with no degree of difficulty)
-1/2 poor
-1 very poor
-1 1/2 extremely poor

PENALTY SCORING

Penalty scores should be assigned each time a penalty occurs. The following deductions will result:

Five Points

Dropping slicker or object required to be carried on course

First or second cumulative refusal, balk, or evading an obstacle by shying or backing

Letting go of gate or dropping rope gate

Use of either hand to instill fear or praise

Falling or jumping off or out of a bridge or a water box with more than one foot once the horse has gottne onto or into that obstacle

Stepping outside of the confines of an obstacle with designated boundaries (i.e., back through, 360-degree box, side pass) with more than one foot once the horse has entered the obstacle

Missing or evading a pole that is a part of a series of an obstacle with more than one foot

Blatant disobedience (including kicking out, bucking, rearing, striking)

Holding the saddle with either hand

Three Points

Incorrect or break of gait at walk or jog for more than two strides

Out of lead or break of gait at lope (except when correcting an incorrect lead)

Knocking down an elevated pole, cone, barrel, or plant obstacle or severely disturbing an obstacle

Falling or jumping off or out of a bridge or a water box with one foot once the horse has entered that obstacle

Stepping outside the confines of, falling out of, or jumping off or out of an obstacle with one foot once horse has entered that obstacle

Missing or evading a pole that is part of a series with one foot

One Point

Each hit, bite, or stepping on a log, pole, plant, cone or any component of the obstacle

Incorrect gait at walk or jog for two strides or less

Both front or hind feet in a single-strided slot or space

Skipping over or failing to step into required space at a walk or jog

Split pole in lope-over

Incorrect number of strides if specified

One-half Point

- Each tick of log, pole, cone, plant, or any component of an obstacle

Zero (0) Score

Use of two hands (except in snaffle bit or hackamore classes designated for two hands) or changing hands on reins, except for junior horses shown with hackamore or snaffle bit, only one hand may be used on the reins although that it is permissible to change hands to work an obstacle or to straighten reins when stopped

Performing the obstacle incorrectly or other than in specified order

No attempt to perform an obstacle

Equipment failure that delays completion of pattern

Excessively or repeatedly touching the horse on the neck to lower the head

Entering or exiting an obstacle from the incorrect side or direction

Working obstacle in the incorrect direction, including overturns of more than one-quarter of a turn

Riding outside designated boundary marker of the arena or course area

Follow QR code for video example of ideal trail horse from the American Paint Horse Association (https://docs.lib.purdue.edu/horseevaluation/6)

Third cumulative refusal, balk, or evading an obstacle by shying or backing

Failure to ever demonstrate correct lead and/or gait as designated

Failure to follow the correct line of travel between obstacles

Excessive schooling, pulling, turning, stepping, or backing anywhere on course

Failure to open and shut gate or failure to complete gate

TRAIL TERMS
- Exhibited more caution and control through the obstacles
- Was more alert and attentive
- Was more relaxed at the gate
- Showed less hesitancy and reluctance
- Was more willfully guided through the course
- Showed more responsiveness to the rider's cues
- Worked a cleaner pattern
- Trotted through the serpentine with more cadence
- Was a calmer, quieter, more responsive individual
- Was relaxed
- Approached each obstacle with more ease and confidence
- Maintained more interest in each task
- Was fault-free
- Was more natural
- Was essentially more correct
- Accumulated fewer penalties through the horse's workman-like approach
- Negotiated the pattern/obstacle with more agility and accuracy
- Was responsive to the rider
- Was more effectively positioned
- Was calm, cool and collected
- Was level-headed
- Was unhurried
- Was untroubled
- Was precise, true, accurate, and exact

- Was easy-moving
- Was sure-footed and alert
- Was quiet over the bridge
- Was cleaner through the trot-overs
- Was truer in the lope-overs
- Was smoother during the back-through
- Lacked the ability, confidence, and cooperation
- Completed the task with fewer obstacle penalties
- Showed more interest
- Listened to the rider's cue
- Was more correct in the length of its stride
- Had more flow
- Was guided more willfully into the chute
- Negotiated the turn with more ease
- Lacked momentum on the approach to the logs during the trot-overs
- Stayed more evenly between the reins
- Moved cleaner through the ground poles
- Accumulated more obstacle points
- Expressed more trail horse talent
- Had better trail horse manners
- Was more pleasing in its obstacle approach and departure
- Worked a cleaner course
- Approached the bridge with more curiosity
- Was more correct in rating its stride over the logs
- Backed through the L with more speed and ease
- Was more careful of its foot placement in the spoke
- Backed smoother through the L
- Side passed more smoothly and correctly
- Was quicker in and out of the box
- Accepted positioning more willingly when working the gate

SAMPLE REASONS: TRAIL

I liked this class of Trail 1-3-2-4. I started with 1, the roan, as he was the most correct in his combination of style, quality, and trail horse talent. He was ridden on a more trusting length of rein while being quieter through the gate and showing less gap to his mouth. Additionally, he maintained a more nearly level frame in his right lope-overs and was a smoother, straighter backing individual who required less adjustment from his rider. Yes, 3 was a more uniform striding individual in the jog-overs. However, 1 was a higher-quality mover who was more even and consistent in his pace from start to finish.

In my intermediate pair I used 3 over 2, as he maintained more forward motion, exhibiting more willingness to execute the left lope-overs with a truer speed and rhythm. He required less handling from the rider, staying more evenly between the reins with a more relaxed poll and supple neck. I won't argue that 2 was more efficient in the 360 box, but he receives several one-point penalties for hits of the logs and was more inconsistent in frame and pace during the lope-overs.

Dropping to my final pair, it was 2 over 4, as 2 was a more stylish performer who passed through the gate with a quieter tail, and he was more accepting of the rider's cues when asked to cross the bridge. Furthermore, he is a longer-striding individual who was softer off his forehand at the lope.

Today 4, the sorrel with the flaxen mane and tail, was my bottom, as he was hesitant over the bridge and busy in his tail and ticked the log coming out of the box. He also received a three-point penalty for breaking gait during the left lead lope. Thank you.

WESTERN HORSEMANSHIP

AQHA HANDBOOK, 2025

Horsemanship is a class in which the western rider and his ability to control his horse are judged.

"Western horsemanship is designed to evaluate the rider's ability to execute, in concert with their horse, a set of maneuvers prescribed by the judge with precision and smoothness while exhibiting poise and confidence and maintaining a balanced, functional and fundamentally correct body position. The ideal horsemanship pattern is extremely precise, with the rider and horse working in complete unison, executing each maneuver with subtle aids and cues. The horse's head and neck should be carried in a relaxed, natural position, with the poll level with or slightly above the withers."

Hand position: Both hands and arms shall be held in a relaxed manner, with the upper arms in a straight line with the body, the one holding the reins bent at the elbow. When using a romal, the rider's off hand shall be around the romal with at least sixteen inches of slack. Some movement of the arm is permissible, but excessive pumping will be penalized. Hands should be around the reins. One finger between the reins is permitted when using split reins but not with a romal. Reins are to be carried immediately above or slightly in front of the saddle horn. Only one hand is to be used for reining and should not be changed. Reins should be carried so as to have light contact with the horse's mouth, and at no time should reins be carried more than a slight hand movement from the horse's mouth. In the event that a horse is shown with a snaffle bit or hackamore, it is permissible for a rider to use two hands on the reins.

Basic body position: Rider should sit in the saddle with their legs hanging straight and slightly forward of the stirrups. The stirrup should be just short enough to allow the heels to be lower than the toes. The rider's body should always appear comfortable, relaxed, and flexible. Feet may be placed home in the stirrup, with the boot heel touching the stirrup, or may be placed less deep in the stirrup. Riding with toes only in the stirrup will be penalized.

Position in motion: Rider should sit to jog-trot and not post. At the lope, the rider should be close to the saddle. All movements of the horse should be governed by the use of imperceptible aids. Exaggerated shifting of the rider's weight is not desirable.

Scoring: Exhibitors are to be scored from 0 to infinity, with 70 denoting an average performance. Patterns will be divided into six to ten maneuvers, as specified by the judge, and each maneuver will be scored from +3 to -3, with 1/2-point increments acceptable that will be added or subtracted from 70.

Maneuver scores should be determined independent of penalties and should reflect equal consideration of both performance of the exhibitor's pattern and the form and effectiveness of the exhibitor and presentation of horse to result in the following scores:

+3 excellent
+2 very good

+1 good
0 average or correct
−1 poor
−2 very poor
−3 extremely poor

Exhibitors' overall form and effectiveness should also be scored from 0 to 5, with 0 to 2 average, 3 good, 4 very good, and 5 excellent. Exhibitors should also be judged on the rail, and their final placing should be adjusted accordingly.

Penalties:
3 Points
- Break of gait at the walk or jog up to two strides
- Over or under turn from one-eighth to one-quarter turn
- Tick or hit of cone

5 Points
- Not performing the specific gait or not stopping within ten feet (three meters) of designated location
- Incorrect lead or break of gait at the lope (except when correcting an incorrect lead)
- Break of gait at walk or jog for more than two strides
- Loss of stirrup
- Bottom of boot not touching pad of stirrup at all gaits including backup
- Head carried too low and/or clearly behind the vertical while the horse is in motion, showing the appearance of intimidation
- Obviously looking down to check leads

10 Points
- Loss of rein
- Use of either hand to instill fear or praise while on pattern or during rail work
- Holding saddle with either hand
- Cueing with the end of the romal
- Blatant disobedience including kicking, pawing, bucking, and rearing
- Spurring in front of the cinch

Disqualifications
- Failure to display the correct number
- Abuse of horse or schooling
- Fall by horse or exhibitor
- Illegal equipment or illegal use of hands on reins
- Use of prohibited equipment
- Off pattern, including knocking over or being on the wrong side of cone or marker, never performing designated gait or lead, over- or underturning more than one-quarter of a turn

WESTERN HORSEMANSHIP TERMS
- Presented the most desirable picture of a horse and rider working in unison, as the rider was more effective and showed her horse to its fullest potential
- Maintained a picture of confidence and control
- Sat taller in the saddle, riding with more style and confidence
- Maintained a smoother and more controlled ride throughout the class
- Carried her or his head up and was more alert, attentive, and confident
- Sat deeper in the saddle with her or his weight more evenly distributed
- Was quieter and deeper-seated
- Was squarer in the shoulders and correctly positioned in the lower back
- Maintained a straighter line from shoulder through hip to heel
- Had more stable and educated hands
- Maintained a horizontal line from bit to elbow
- Showed smoother and more effective execution of the aids, showing more adaptability, sympathy, and control with her or his hands
- Had a more secure leg that maintained closer contact with the sides of the horse, allowing the rider to be discrete with her or his aids
- Had a stronger, more effective leg with more angulation to the heel
- Stayed with the horse and sat transitions more smoothly

SAMPLE REASONS: WESTERN HORSEMANSHIP

I placed this Western Horsemanship class 1-3-4-2, finding the 1 gave a more complete picture of horse and rider working in unison. In my top pair, I placed 1 over 3 because the confident rider on the dun displayed more elegant and correct posture and maintained a picture of confidence and control. Furthermore, she was squarer in her shoulders yet more relaxed in her back, allowing her to more easily absorb the concussion of the horse's motion. I grant that 3 had more correct angulation to the heel, but it was 1 who maintained a smoother and more controlled ride throughout the class.

Moving to my middle pair, I placed 3 over 4 because the girl on the sorrel executed her aids with more discretion and was quieter and more stable in her hands. Furthermore, she had a more secure leg that maintained closer contact with the sides of the horse, allowing her to be discrete with her aids. I readily admit that 4 sat deeper in the saddle; however, it was 3 who was smoother and more effective in cueing her horse and more proper in her hand movement.

Advancing to my final pair, I placed 4 over 2 because 4 carried more weight in her heel and sat transitions more smoothly, and her horse backed the most correctly of any in the class. I grant that 2, the girl riding the bay, carried her head up more; however, it was 4 who had a steadier seat at the jog and lope. Realizing that 2 was squarer in her shoulders, I nonetheless must fault her and placed her at the bottom of the class because she did not display balance or control, turned her toes out too far, pulled excessively at her horse's mouth at the jog and lope, and lacked the overall balance, control, and poise to merit a higher placing in this class today. Thank you.

WESTERN PLEASURE

A western pleasure animal is a sensible, alert, bright, easy-moving, well-mannered mount that can provide a quiet, comfortable, and pleasant ride.

Western pleasure is shown at a walk, jog, and lope in both directions of the ring.

Horses are required to back easily and stand readily. A good pleasure horse has a stride of reasonable length in keeping with his conformation. The horse has enough cushion to its, pastern to give the rider a pleasant, smooth ride. The horse should move lightly in the front with its hocks well up underneath it, exhibiting a great deal of hindquarter impulsion combined with cadence and collection. The horse has relatively flat knees. High, round motion is to be penalized. The horse carries its head in a natural position, not high with the nose out or low and overflexed at the poll. Credit should be given to a horse that is relaxed but has its ears alert, looks balanced in its way of going, and is bright as well as responsive to the reins. When asked to extend the jog or lope, the horse moves out with the same smooth way of going.

The walk is a natural, flat-footed, four-beat gait. The horse must move straight and true at the walk. The walk must be alert, with a stride of reasonable length in keeping with the size of the horse.

The jog is a smooth ground-covering two-beat diagonal gait. The horse works from one pair of diagonals to the other pair. The jog should be square and balanced, with a straight, forward movement of the feet. Horses walking with their back feet and jogging on the front are not considered to be performing the required gait and should be penalized accordingly.

The lope is an easy, rhythmical, three-beat gait. Horses moving to the left should lope on the left lead, while horses moving to the right should lope on the right lead.

Horses traveling at a four-beat gait are not considered to be performing a proper lope and should be penalized significantly. The horse should lope with a natural stride and appear relaxed and smooth. The horse should be ridden at a speed that is a natural way of going.

The western pleasure horse should carry its head and neck in a relaxed, natural position, with its poll level with or slightly above the level of the withers. The horse should not carry its head behind the vertical, giving the appearance of intimidation, or be excessively nosed out, giving a resistant appearance. The western pleasure horse should be shown on a reasonably loose yet controlled, rein. The horse should be responsive and smooth in its transitions. Maximum credit should be given to the flowing, balanced, and willing horse that gives the appearance of being fit and a pleasure to ride. There will be some breed variation in way of going in western pleasure horses. Arabians, Saddlebreds, Morgans, and Tennessee Walking Horses will display more flexion of the knees and higher carriage of the head than the stock type breeds. These breeds should be evaluated compared to their breed standard in these areas.

WESTERN PLEASURE TERMS
- Walk
- Jog
- Lope
- Brokeness
- Broke and honest
- Required less handling
- Had a softer foot-to-ground contact
- Was a more broke individual
- Reversed with less bridle-rein contact
- Worked at a more desirable speed
- Required less checking on the part of the rider
- Was lower in its frame, allowing the horse to be flatter and more forward in its movement
- Was a more solid, quieter individual that works the pen in a calmer fashion as it has a more polished . . .

Follow QR code for video example of excellent gaits in a stock-type western pleasure horse (https://docs.lib.purdue.edu/horseevaluation/7)

- Required less hand-to-mouth contact
- Was capable of easier handling
- Had more industry-preferred head and neck positioning, style, and movement
- Traveled on a longer, looser rein
- Showed a higher degree of responsiveness
- Was more consistent about its head, neck, and shoulder positions
- Carried its head more perpendicular to the ground, with more flexion at the poll
- Yielded more to the bridle when asked to back
- More correct or industry-preferred face placement
- Appeared to have a softer mouth with more feel
- Maintained a more nearly level frame during its smoother transitions
- Had a more desirable head carriage, showing more flexion at the poll and looking straighter through the bridle
- Was more mindful of the bit as it carries its head more correctly
- Was more even and upright in its shoulder positioning
- Showed more shoulder freedom
- Had a more rounded spine
- Had more arc to the spine
- Was stronger over the back, allowing the horse to be deeper hocked
- Had more of an upward arc from wither to hip, allowing the horse to be deeper behind
- Had more hind quarter impulsion
- Was deeper loping
- Was tighter in its croup and hock
- Had more hind leg sweep when at the lope
- Rolled its hips less at the jog
- Had more hind leg engagement
- Maintained tighter tail placement
- Lifted its loin, drove with its hocks, and thus was a deeper-loping individual
- Was tighter hocked
- Was more correctly hinged in the shoulder and hip and consequently lifted his back more, thus enabling the horse to step off into the lope with a deeper hock
- Higher-quality mover, being flatter kneed, squarer jogging, and deeper hocked at the lope

- Was a flashier mover, as the horse slips across the ground lower and leveler at the walk, jog, and lope
- Lifted its loin while driving off its hocks, allowing the horse to take a deeper step behind
- Drove deeper into all four corners
- Was a flatter-kneed, squarer-jogging, deeper-loping individual who was more preferred in its frame, being rounder in the spine and more correctly broken at the wither and poll
- Had more western pleasure talent
- Was squarer jogging and more fluid at the lope
- Exhibited less elevation to knee and hock
- Had more depth of step behind at the jog
- Was squarer and more elevated through the forehand and thus hinged more effectively through the shoulder, allowing the horse to have more flatness and flow in front
- Moved with more drive off its hocks, thus adding a higher degree of difficulty moving down the rail with a longer, more efficient stride
- Slipped down the rail with a longer, more fluid stride

SAMPLE REASONS: WESTERN PLEASURE

I liked this class of Western Pleasure, 2-1-3-4. I started today with 2, as he was the most correct in his combination of brokeness, quality of motion, and western pleasure talent. The chestnut was ridden on a more forgiving rein, was more relaxed in his poll, was supple in his neck, and was more responsive to the rider, requiring less adjustment. I won't argue that 1 tracked deeper underneath himself at the lope, but I opted to leave him second because he required more handling throughout the class.

Moving to my intermediate pair, I used 1 over 3, as he was a slower-legged individual who was more correctly hinged in the shoulder and hip and consequently lifted his back more, thus enabling him to step off into the lope with a deeper hock. Sure, 1 was steadier over his topline, but he was shallow-hocked behind and heavy on his forehand, causing him to have a four-beat lope.

Dropping to my final pair, it is a matter of consistency and brokeness, placing 3 over 4, as 3 was smoother and more accepting of all his transitions and was freer from breaking while loping to the right. Yes, 4 took a deeper step behind; however, 3 was a squarer-jogging individual who kept a more consistent pace and rhythm both ways of the pen.

Today 4, the bay, is my bottom, as he was the least broke individual who required the most handling during his transitions. He broke gait while at the lope and was the highest-headed, tightest-reined horse of the four. Thank you.

WESTERN RIDING

AQHA HANDBOOK, 2025

The western riding horse is judged on quality of gaits, lead changes at the lope, response to the rider, manners, and disposition. The horse should perform with reasonable speed and be sensible, well-mannered, and free- and easy-moving. Credit shall be given for and emphasis placed on smoothness, even cadence of gaits (i.e., starting and finishing pattern with the same cadence), and the horse's ability to change leads precisely, easily, and simultaneously both hind and front at the center point between markers. In order to have balance, with quality lead changes, the horse's head and neck should be in a relaxed, natural position, with its poll level with or slightly above the level of the withers.

SCORING WESTERN RIDING

Scoring will be on a basis of 0–100, with 70 denoting an average performance. Just as in reining, scoring western riding horses is divided into maneuver scoring and standardized penalty scoring. The final score is a combination of the two.

MANEUVER SCORING

Points will be added or subtracted from the nine maneuvers on the following basis, ranging from plus 1 1/2 points for an excellent maneuver to minus 1 1/2 points for an extremely poor maneuver:

+1 1/2 excellent
+1 very good
+1/2 good
0 average (maneuver performed correctly but with no degree of difficulty)
−1/2 poor
−1 very poor
−1 1/2 extremely poor

PENALTY SCORING

Penalty scores are assigned for specific infractions. A penalty score and a maneuver score can both be assigned when appropriate. A contestant shall be penalized each time the following occurs:

Five Points

- Out of lead beyond the next designated change area. (Note: failures to change, including cross-cantering. Two consecutive failures to change would result in two five-point penalties.)
- Blatant disobedience, including kicking out, biting, bucking, and rearing
- Holding the saddle with either hand
- Use of either hand to instill fear or praise

Three Points

- Not performing the specific gait (jog or lope) or not stopping when called for in the pattern within ten feet (three meters) of the designated area
- Simple change of leads
- Out of lead at or before the marker prior to the designated change area or out of lead at or after the marker after the designated change area
- Additional lead changes anywhere in the pattern (except when correcting an extra change or incorrect lead)
- In patterns one and six and Level 1 patterns one and six, failure to start the lope within thirty feet (nine meters) after crossing the log at the jog
- Break of gait at walk or jog for more than two strides
- Break of gait at the lope

One Point

- Hitting or rolling the log

- Out of lead more than one stride on either the side of the center point and between the markers
- Splitting the log (log between the two front or two hind feet) at the lope
- Break of gait at the walk or jog up to two strides
- Nonsimultaneous lead change (front to hind or hind to front) or hind legs skipping or coming together during lead change

One-half Point
- Tick or light touch of the log

Disqualified: 0 Score
- Illegal equipment
- Willful abuse
- Off-course
- Knocking over markers
- Completely missing the log
- Major refusal (stop and back more than two strides or four steps with front legs)
- Major disobedience or schooling
- Failure to start lope prior to end cone
- Four or more simple lead changes and/or failures to change leads
- Failure to start lope beyond thirty feet of designated area in patterns 2, 3, 4, 5 7, 8, and 9 and Level 1 western riding patterns 1, 2, 4, 7 and 9 (except for Level 1 classes)
- Overturn of more than one-quarter of a turn

Faults that should be scored according to severity:
- Head carried too low (tip of ear consistently below withers)
- Overflexing or straining the neck in head carriage so that the nose is carried behind the vertical consistently

Credits:
- Changes of leads, hind and front simultaneously
- Change of lead near the center point of the lead change area
- Accurate and smooth pattern
- Even pace throughout
- Easy to guide and control with rein and leg
- Manners and disposition
- Conformation and fitness

Faults to be judged in maneuver scores:
- Opening mouth excessively
- Anticipating signals
- Stumbling
- Carrying head too high
- Carrying head too low (tip of ear consistently below the withers)

- Overflexing or straining neck in head carriage so the nose is carried behind the vertical
- Excessive nosing out

WESTERN RIDING TERMS
- Maintained a more consistent pace from start to finish
- Was a flashier mover
- Kept in frame as it maneuvered the line changes with ease
- Was easiest, freest-moving, and the most stylish
- Maneuvered the pattern in a smoother manner
- Was concurrent in its changes
- Had fewer penalties
- Was more correct in the placement of its lead changes
- Changed more precisely in between the cones
- Loped over the log with ease
- Had fewer refusals
- Was calm, cool, and collected
- Was unhurried in its changes, maintaining its same pace
- Moved easily throughout the pattern
- Was quiet and untroubled
- Appeared natural
- Was level-headed
- Lacked the ability, confidence, and cooperation
- Was accurate, true, and exact
- Was more pleasant in its attitude and showed less anticipation
- Was smoother in its changes
- Was more forward in its changes
- Was less animated in its changes
- Showed less resentment
- Needed less dictation to change leads
- Was more balanced in its changes
- Was flatter in its changes
- Showed more pattern desirability
- Was flatter and more forward in its lead changes
- Was more correct in its placement of lead changes
- Showed more pattern symmetry
- Required less handling throughout the pattern
- Was more correct over the log
- Was more correct in its pattern position
- Showed more uniformity to its pattern
- Was more correct in the positioning of its lead changes
- Showed more communication between the horse and the rider
- Stayed more upright in its shoulders

- Exhibited less pylon pushing
- Was simultaneous in both its line and crossing changes
- Was cleaner over the log
- Covered the log both times with more ease
- Maintained a more consistent pace throughout the pattern
- Was smoother in its transitions
- Showed less anticipation
- Was more exact in the placement of its transitions
- Required less dictation to change leads
- Was quieter through its ears and tail through its lead changes
- Placed its changes more effectively between the cones
- Maintained more forward motion through its changes
- Was a more willing lead changer
- Was more effortless throughout all changes
- Required less of an effort from the rider
- Was more correctly hinged in the shoulder and hip, resulting in more hang time
- Was more positive in its ears and quieter in its tail

SAMPLE REASONS: WESTERN RIDING

I liked this class of Western Riding 1-2-3-4. I started with 1, the bay, as he was more correct in his combination of pattern precision, consistency, and brokeness. In relation to 2, 1 was a flashier mover who kept in frame more as he maneuvered the line, with flatter and more forward changes that were more precise in their placement between the cones. I won't dispute the fact that 2 gave more to the bridle while backing. However, he goes second as he required more handling down the line and came up out of frame during his changes.

Moving to my intermediate pair, I used 2 over 3, as he was cleaner over the log at the jog, maintaining a more consistent pace throughout the pattern with a quieter tail. Yes, 3 was a smoother-stopping individual, but he receives two one-point penalties for non-simultaneous changes as well as a half point penalty for ticking the jog log.

Dropping to my final pair, I used 3 over 4 simply because 3 was a more fundamentally correct individual who accumulated fewer penalty deductions, being freer from disobedience. He held his body straighter while changing leads, staying more relaxed in his face and poll, and was ridden on a longer and more giving rein.

Today 4 is my bottom, as he received the most penalty points. He had a five-point deduction for kicking out and was a tight-reined individual who was on the muscle, behind the vertical, and crooked in his body while changing and came out of the bridle and was resistant when asked to stop. Thank you.

3

ORAL REASONS

PHILOSOPHY FOR GIVING ORAL REASONS

Oral reasons are one of the most important skills gained through participation in youth judging contests. Giving oral reasons helps students develop critical thinking, organize their thoughts, and articulate them in a structured environment. These skills are valuable in various aspects of life. Many leaders in the animal science industry attribute their leadership skills to their experience on judging teams, particularly the practice of giving oral reasons. Research from Purdue University highlights that participants in 4-H judging programs found these programs instrumental in enhancing their ability to verbally defend decisions, improve oral communication, make decisions, and boost self-confidence. Most individuals involved in competitive youth judging report that giving oral reasons was one of the most beneficial parts of the program.

It is not unusual for people to find giving oral reasons uncomfortable and to feel anxious about preparing and presenting reasons, especially when they first begin judging. Public speaking can be intimidating for many people. In fact, research says that as many as 75% of people have a fear of public speaking, and some people report being more afraid of public speaking than of death. Therefore, coaches should provide constructive feedback to help judges overcome their reluctance to give oral reasons and reassure participants that being anxious is normal and that they can work through it as they develop their skills, just as they work through concerns about development of other skills. One successful strategy is to have participants focus on the format of their reasons and start with simple sets of reasons following the basic format and then gradually increase the details and complexity of their sets as their confidence grows.

MAJOR CRITERIA FOR REASONS

ORGANIZATION

Styles of reasons vary with individual personalities and coaching tactics, but all reasons should be well organized. The basic approach involves comparing animals in three pairs: the top pair, the middle pair, and the bottom pair. Reasons should be comparative rather than descriptive. For example, instead of saying "1 had a short back," say "1 had a shorter back than 2." As the reasons giver gains confidence, adding transition sentences between pairs and more detailed comparison in the body of the reasons is useful.

RELEVANCY

Reasons should reflect the actual differences in the pair and focus on the primary points significant in the placing. Higher scores are given for reasons that emphasize the most important criteria used in making the placing decision. When reasons givers are inexperienced, focusing on the one or two most important points in the placing should be included. It can be helpful to look back at the criteria for each class to help determine what those most important factors are. If reasons sound memorized and are inconsistent with the true differences in the horses, they may be identified as "canned" and receive reduced scores, so how smoothly they are delivered matters.

ACCURACY

Correctness in reporting observations is crucial. While omitting relevant information may result in minor penalties, inaccurate statements are severely penalized. Again, the emphasis should be placed on the major criteria for placing the class. Add the minor criteria as the reasons giver gets more confident and is ready to give a longer set of reasons. A complete and accurate set of reasons should receive a high score even if the student's placing differs from the official placing. The student and the official may prioritize the importance of specific observations differently, but they should agree on the observed characteristics.

TERMINOLOGY

Terminology should reflect common usage among horsemen and be comparative rather than descriptive, using "-er" and "-est" words between pairs. Avoid noninformative words such as "nice" and "good," which don't tell the reasons listener what was observed. For example, instead of says "horse 1 had a nicer neck than 2," say "horse 1 had a longer neck than 2." A set of reasons that consistently describes traits instead of comparing them will be penalized.

PRESENTATION

Oral reasons should be presented confidently and convincingly, without arrogance. Loud, boisterous delivery is penalized, while shy, timid reasons won't receive the highest score either. Reasons should be given in a relaxed, conversational manner with smooth flow. The judge should stand comfortably, with weight balanced and hands quietly behind the back. Avoid swaying, rocking, or otherwise shifting weight from foot to foot. If this is a challenge, standing with the feet slightly offset will help reduce the likelihood of weight shifting. Reasons should be delivered within two minutes, with correct grammar, pronunciation, and enunciation. Reasons that exceed two minutes will be penalized.

HINTS FOR COMPETITION

Many coaches/participants find it useful to write out sets of reasons. Be cautious about memorizing complete sets of reasons. It is most effective to memorize why the placing was made and the most important criteria rather than a word-for-word written set. The challenge with memorizing an entire set of reasons is that if the reasons giver forgets a word or a phrase, this often results in forgetting the remainder of the set. It may be useful to try to picture the horses in your head while preparing and practicing your reasons so that you can call them to your mind when giving a set of reasons. Refer to the terms throughout this manual for suggestions of terminology and transition phrases appropriate for different classes.

When practicing reasons sets, practice the complete set. Do not stop and start over every time you make a mistake. There are two reasons for this. (1) You need to practice how you will handle it if you make a mistake in the reasons room. (2) If you stop every time you make a mistake, you will practice the first pair many times and the last pair the fewest times. By going through the full set each time you practice, the entire set will be equally prepared.

Practice, practice, practice. The key to giving good sets of reasons is to practice. Practice out loud and in your head. Practice in the car. Practice when you are waiting for something. Practice made-up sets of reasons to get used to using different terminology and phrases. Do not practice only with your coach and team. Anyone can listen to a set of reasons and give you a chance to practice talking to a real person. Good luck!!

SCORING ORAL REASONS

Scores should reflect the organization, relevancy, accuracy, terminology, and presentation of reasons, regardless of the contestant's actual placing. If a contestant's placing differs from the official's, accurate and supportive reasons can still receive a good score. This is an important point to make to participants as they are preparing. If they believe in their placing and can support their placing with their reasons, they can often make up for any points lost in the placing portion of the contest.

GUIDELINES FOR ASSIGNING SCORES

- **Good to excellent:** 46–50
- **Above average to Good:** 41–45
- **Average:** 36–40
- **Below average:** 31–35
- **Poor:** 30 and below

A reasonably prepared contestant who presents a complete set of reasons from memory in the correct general format should never score less than 25. Contestants who read their notes should be severely penalized, with a score of 20 being generous. The contest coordinator should make clear to reasons listeners how they want read reasons to be scored and make the same clear to the coaches and the participants. That will make it very clear to the coaches and the participants when they see the final contest scores how read reasons were scored. Even the best-read set should never score higher than the worst complete set of reasons presented by memory.

REASONS ORGANIZATION: 10 POINTS

Reasons should start with an introductory statement identifying the class and selected placings. This identification of the class should be specific and include the breed and the sex in halter classes. It is good practice to use the same class title as was announced at the contest. Refer to the sample reasons throughout the manual for examples of different introductory statements. The contestant should then move through each pair with introductory and supporting statements that compare the pairs, including faults and grants. Contestants may develop an individual style that reflects their personality and viewpoint, but organization should remain consistent. Some organizational styles do not include faults in the intermediate pairs and only fault the last horse. It is important to focus on the positive in the horses that are being judged and not get carried away with the faults. Often, faults in one horse can be changed into credits for another horse. For example, if horse 3 is over at the knees, instead of faulting 3 for being over at the knees, you can credit the horse you are comparing it to for being more correct in the alignment of its knees.

DELIVERY: 10 POINTS

The reasons giver should have a neat appearance, stand relaxed but alert with good posture, and speak clearly with a controlled, convincing voice. Voice variation can emphasize key points, but shouting is penalized. The reasons listener should be able to easily hear the set of reasons.

CONTENT: 25 POINTS

Content quality is crucial, constituting of 50% of the total score. Content must be accurate and applicable, with major penalties for inaccuracies. The terminology examples offered throughout this manual will be useful in helping to accurately reflect the observations of the judger. It is better to have a shorter, more accurate and precise set of reasons than a longer set of reasons that may have inaccuracies.

VOCABULARY: 5 POINTS

Correct terminology and grammar are necessary for a high score. Using a variety of terms throughout the reasons will result in a higher score. It is frequently useful to find terms, phrases, and transitions that you are comfortable with and use them consistently. However, make sure they are always accurate for the class you are talking about.

TOTAL: 50 POINTS

REASONS LISTENERS

Listeners must be aware that their actions can significantly affect students. Judges should be polite and encouraging, avoiding harsh criticism and distracting movements. In contests, listeners should score contestants without providing clinics. Feedback can be given through notes to the contest coordinator for distribution after the contest.

UNDERSTANDING AND ASSIGNING CUTS

Cuts assign numerical values to the difficulty of decisions between animals. Higher cuts indicate easier decisions, while lower cuts indicate difficult decisions. Cuts are used to calculate the final score, out of 50, by deducting points for each incorrect placing. At a judging contest, the final placing of a class is generally set by a panel of official judges, and that panel will also determine the cuts. If the cut is small, it may indicate that even the officials did not agree on the placing of that pair. The guidelines for assigning cuts are as follows:

- **Cut of 1:** Horses are extremely similar. Placing is a matter of personal preference.
- **Cut of 2:** Horses are close, with a few advantages; half of the contestants could logically switch the pair.
- **Cut of 3:** Horses are similar, but one has several advantages. No more than one-third of contestants would switch the pair.
- **Cut of 4:** Horses are not similar. One has several advantages. No more than 10% of contestants would switch the pair.
- **Cut of 5:** Horses have large differences. Placing is obvious. Only inexperienced contestants would switch the pair.
- **Cut of 6:** Horses are not comparable. Differences reflect champion quality versus nonshow quality.
- **Cut of 7:** This is the largest cut. Differences reflect world-class versus poor-quality or lame horses.

FIGURING PLACING SCORES

Although there are apps available for calculating placing scores, it is useful to also understand how to mathematically figure placing scores. This will also allow the judger to have a better understanding of how the app/computer program came to their final score.

When manually calculating the score, you compare how the officials placed each horse to how the contestant placed it. If they are different, the value of the cuts is deducted from the perfect score of 50. For our examples the officials are as follows:

- **Official:** 4-2-1-3, cuts of 2, 3, 5. Perfect score is 50.

EXAMPLE 1

- **Contestant placing:** 4-1-2-3

Ask a series of yes/no questions using the official placing as the guide. If the answer is yes, there is no point deduction. If the answer is no, write down the number of the cut(s), and that is what will be deducted.

Is 4 placed over 2? Yes, no point deduction.
Is 4 placed over 1? Yes, no point deduction.
Is 4 placed over 3? Yes, no point deduction.
Is 2 placed over 1? No, deduct 3 points.
Is 2 placed over 3? Yes, no point deduction.
Is 1 placed over 3? Yes, no point deduction.

After you have made all of the comparisons, add up the number of points deducted and subtract from 50 for the final score. In this example, the final score is 47.

Follow QR code for video example showing how to manually calculate contestant score from placing a class (https://docs.lib.purdue.edu/horseevaluation/8)

EXAMPLE 2

- **Contestant placing:** 2-4-3-1
  Is 4 placed over 2? No, 2 point deduction.
  Is 4 placed over 1? Yes, no point deduction.
  Is 4 placed over 3? Yes, no point deduction.
  Is 2 placed over 1? Yes, no point deduction.
  Is 2 placed over 3? Yes, no point deduction.
  Is 1 placed over 3? No, 5 point deduction.

Total point deduction of 7 points, with final score of 43.

EXAMPLE 3

- **Contestant placing:** 4-3-2-1
  Is 4 placed over 2? Yes, no point deduction.
  Is 4 placed over 1? Yes, no point deduction.
  Is 4 placed over 3? Yes, no point deduction.
  Is 2 placed over 1? Yes, no point deduction.
  Is 2 placed over 3? No, 8 point deduction. (There is a 3-point cut and a 5-point cut between the official placing and the contestant placing of 3, so there is an 8 point deduction.)
  Is 1 placed over 3? No, 5 point deduction.

Total point deduction of 13 points, final score 37.

EXAMPLE 4

- **Contestant placing:** 3-4-1-2
  Is 4 placed over 2? Yes, no point deduction.
  Is 4 placed over 1? Yes, no point deduction.
  Is 4 placed over 3? No, 10 point deduction.
  Is 2 placed over 1? No, 3 point deduction.

Is 2 placed over 3? No, 8 point deduction.
Is 1 placed over 3? No, 5 point deduction.

Total point deduction 26, final score 24.

Try calculating scores with the provided examples. Check your scores against the calculations of a scoring app.

Official: 2-1-4-3
Cuts: 3, 3, 4
Perfect score: 50

Contestant placing #1, 1-4-3-2
Contestant placing #2, 2-1-3-4
Contestant placing #3, 3-2-1-4
Contestant placing #4, 4-2-3-1

ABOUT THE AUTHOR

COLLEEN BRADY is a professor and extension specialist at Purdue University, where she specializes in equine science and youth development. With a passion for horses that began in childhood, Brady earned a PhD in animal science and has since gained extensive experience in competitive horse judging. For the past twenty-five years, she has dedicated her career to educating and mentoring the next generation of horse enthusiasts and professionals, focused on youth horse judging education. She has conducted live and virtual horse judging camps and worked with a team of collaborators to develop online horse-judging materials. She remains committed to fostering a deep appreciation for horses of all breeds and disciplines, and encourages students to value lifelong learning and the relationships built through participation in horse-judging activities.

www.ingramcontent.com/pod-product-compliance
Lightning Source LLC
Chambersburg PA
CBHW080739230426
43665CB00020B/2800